Married to the Game
A Story of Love and Waiting

Married to the Game
A Story of Love and Waiting

Lydia Harris

Published by:
L. B. Publishing
14019 S. W. Freeway
Suite 599
Sugarland, Texas 77478

Copyright © 2005 Lydia Harris
Interior text design by Tom Davis
Edited by Ellis Harrington
ISBN: 0-9765660-0-1
Library of Congress Control Number: 2005929729

Married to the Game.
All rights reserved. Except for brief excerpts used in reviews, no portion of this work may be reproduced or published without expressed written permission from the author or the author's agent.

First Edition
Printed and bound in the United States of America by Morris Publishing • www.morrispublishing.com • 800-650-7888
1 2 3 4 5 6 7 8 9 10

Foreword

This book is based on the life experiences of Lydia Harris, wife of convicted drug kingpin Michael "Harry O" Harris and mother of his daughter, and is a tale of love, loyalty, deceit, and betrayal. You will, without doubt, be captured by its pages. This book will show you how one woman has survived being in the trenches with some of the music industry's most notorious villains. It will also highlight her loyalty to the man she loved during a crucial time of state and federal court proceedings.

As a former executive of Lifestyle Records, I've seen firsthand the tribulations and enduring pain of Lydia Harris. I know that the various movers and shakers in Hollywood did not want to see her make it in the business. They thought that she was naive and wouldn't claim her fair share of the enormous profits generated by her partnership with her husband. Well, in the end it will be proven that she's no flake.

Despite the many lies and scare tactics she encountered during her tenure with the company, Lydia Harris stood tall and survived the test of time. Married to the

Game is an eye opener and will ultimately prove how character, determination, and a creative mind have prevailed over an evil empire of mistrust and greed.

– Greg Cross

CONTENTS

Act One	9
Life Without	13
Front Row, Seat 3	21
The Nightmare and the Dream	29
Low Profile	35
Women!	39
And One Woman in Particular	45
An Unholy War	55
How it Works	61
Checkmate	63
Psycho/Analyzing	69
What the Papers Say	71
Play the Game, and the Game Plays You	77
What You Don't Understand	85
The Federal Probe	89
Bringing Color to the Great White Way	95
Squeeze Play	109
Listen to the Man	121
Stranded	125
...And If I Hadn't Married the Game	127
The Buzz	131
Making Good	143
Testimony	145
What Money Won't Buy	147
The Evolution of Me	149
All My Children	175
Taking off the Gloves	177

Words to Live by 187
Words *I've* Lived by 189
And, at Last: Revelations 191
Acknowledgments 195
About the Author 199

ACT ONE

I wasn't born for drama. In fact, I was a little bit of the girl next door. Coming from Houston, Texas, and a strong, committed family, I just happened to meet, fall in love with, and marry someone that many people would consider "the wrong kind of man." But luckily (and mercifully) for me – my mother, Mary Robinson, has always supported my decisions, my marriage, and my husband Mike. Oh, certainly she's been afraid for me, and worried. Yet somehow she trusted Mike's judgments and his opinions and his love for me. She set aside her own life to help rear our daughter LyDasia. And she has provided for us a loving, wholesome, healthy, *normal* family life. She's the kindness, the sacrifice, the devotion, and the miracle. Without her there is no story..

"I have determined what's important in my life by staying true to myself, not losing focus, and remembering the people and the things that make me happy."

– My pledge to myself

LIFE WITHOUT

Can you imagine fifteen years, or twenty, of being married but alone? Can anybody? Well, neither could I. And it wasn't my choice, but it's been my reality.

My husband Michael has been incarcerated since 1988. During this very long time he has been moved around from Soledad to Pelican Bay to Lancaster State and Tehachapi, all in California. I've seen him at least a couple of thousand times, but always at these prisons. He hasn't been home with me at Thanksgiving or Christmas, or on my birthday, or to celebrate Valentine's Day or our anniversary. I've traveled to too many court hearings, on planes or trains or in cars, and I've stayed in drab and lonesome hotels. And Michael and

I are parents only because Lancaster State Prison allowed conjugal visits. We haven't had a storybook marriage. *You* may think we haven't had marriage at all!

Michael Harris, also known as Harry O, is serving a twenty-eight-years-to-life sentence for attempted murder. He was also convicted on federal charges of money laundering and conspiracy in one of the biggest drug busts in California history. He wasn't a saint, and in fact he was one of the most "successful" cocaine traffickers in the United States during the 1980s. However, he was also an innovative, talented, legitimate businessman and the co-founder of one of the most powerful music labels in recent history, Death Row Records, which became the home of West Coast hip-hop. He is a magnificent contradiction in terms.

It's no secret, and it's a tragedy, that many young Black men in America have destroyed their lives, their families, and their considerable potential with drugs and violence. They've victimized other people, obviously, and they've *been* victims – of low expectations, of low-income hopelessness, of their own shortcomings, of history and media hype and racial profiling, and of the streets. The lack of legitimate opportunities in Black urban society is what Michael calls "slave economics," and, yes, he profited from it. It's a complicated thing, and I doubt that it's going away because it's everywhere

Married to the Game

and because it's incredibly attractive to many, many young African-American males.

But there's another ugly variation on Black society, and it's the destination of those who become too intelligent, too powerful, too successful – too fearsome. Although the situation sounds like a bad movie, it's not an exaggeration. What it *is* is a belief that the intelligent, the powerful, and the successful must be stopped, that they must be silenced; and often they are. People have tried to silence Michael Harris. They've tried to silence me. My life has been threatened. My home has been burglarized. My dog was shot and killed. No longer able to feel safe in houses and apartments, I began living in hotel rooms, under aliases, and I've had bodyguards. I became afraid even for my daughter's safety and could not allow her to live with me. Instead, our relationship has been a daily 5:00 AM phone call, wrapped around my guilt and sadness, and our love. I absolutely know the meaning of "for better or worse." And the cast of characters in my life is nothing if not interesting:

- Prison guards
- Business associates carrying glocks and .38 specials
- Crooked lawyers
- Crooked cops

- Gangstas and gang-bangers
- Greedy music-industry CEOs
- Performers with talent, and without

Some of the names transcend the world of rap music:

- Denzel Washington
- Vanessa Willams
- Earvin "Magic" Johnson
- Dionne Warwick
- Marla Gibbs
- William Bennett, former Drug Czar and U.S. Secretary of Education
- Senator Bob Dole

Others have everything to do with rap:

- Marion "Suge" Knight
- Tupac Shakur
- Rap-a-Lot founder James "Li'l J" Smith
- Eazy E
- NWA and its manager, Jerry Heller
- Snoop Dogg
- Warren G
- Mary J. Blige

Married to the Game

- Interscope's Jimmy Iovine and Ted Fields
- RED Sony's Alan Greenblatt
- Dr. Dre
- Convicted tax evader (and my former attorney) David Kenner
- Clive Davis, chairman and creator of Arista Records
- Doug Morris, chairman of MCA/Universal Music and ex-head of Atlantic Records
- Sylvia Rhone, first and only Black female head of a major music label (Elektra)
- Edgar Bronfman, Jr., owner of Universal Studios, Putnam Publishing, MCA...
- John T. McClain, who advanced the careers of Janet Jackson, Blackstreet's Teddy Riley, and Ice Cube, and who gave Death Row a break at Interscope
- Dick Griffey, chairman of Solar Records (home of The Whispers, Baby Face, and The Dells)
- Kevin Black, street promoter for Death Row, Virgin, and A&M

Obviously, none of the names, the faces, or the companies have kept me warm or comfortable or happy. None of them has been a substitute for a husband, a home, or a constant, genuine family life. But they probably say plenty about me. They probably explain something about why I'm who I am. They can probably help introduce you to Lydia Harris.

"Lydia Harris is Winnie Mandela to me because she stayed down, and not too many women have the self-discipline and sacrifice to stay down with a brother who is incarcerated."

– Former LA gang member

FRONT ROW, SEAT 3

There's no such thing as a comfortable courtroom bench. This I know. For two years – two years! – I held vigil at the Metropolitan Detention Center in Los Angeles while Michael was being tried on federal charges. Early on, I had resolved to stay with him, by his side, throughout our lives. I was devoted to him and to our marriage. Some days were hard, though – as hard as those courtroom benches and as grim as the prison visitation areas. Some days conspired to make me quit, though I never did.

The prospect of a business meeting at Mickey D's jarred my memory and took me back to the beginning, to a time of innocent excitement over my relationship with Michael Harris and innocent expectations of where life might be planning to take us. Mike wanted me to meet an acquaintance from the old neighborhood – from South Central California, which he refers to as "The Low Bottoms." The acquaintance was Marion "Suge" Knight, who was interested in our brand new company, Death Row Records. The meeting was to be simple enough, but somehow it served up memories of how it felt to be me when I'd still believed in America's justice system, before my husband's high-profile problems, before I'd ever even met anybody who wasn't a law-abiding citizen. I who had never received so much as a slap on the wrist for jay-walking was suddenly spending time with criminal-law attorneys, working on defense strategies, and becoming Michael's contact with the outside world.

I had gotten to know Dee, who would be at the meeting with Suge, after his release from the prison where he'd met Mike. They were from the same neighborhood, and Mike – who at that time was still in his twenties – was considered by younger guys like Dee to be an elder statesman on the streets. Dee had been sent up after he and a friend were arrested by federal agents for transporting AK-47s, if not *to*, then at least *toward* the Super Bowl. So Mike and Dee met in prison, and Mike took the young man from the old neighborhood under his wing. As Michael said, "I guess it's just a Low Bottoms thing."

Anyway, I found myself worrying about the upcoming meeting. I was scared, though I couldn't have said *why*. I do remember thinking, "What have I gotten myself into?" But then there we were – Suge, Dee, Kim (also known as "Paradise"), a handful of other folks, and me – and, sure enough, this would be the first time that I would experience Suge's unpredictable and intimidating behavior.

We made it through the meeting okay, I thought, but just barely. As we were leaving the building, Suge said something disrespectful to Dee and immediately drew his fist back to hit him. Now, Suge, who's 6'5", weighed at least three hundred pounds then, and Dee was a fraction of his size — 5'8", maybe 175 pounds – so it was only logical that he start running. In fact, he ran right out of his shoes! But once he reached his car, and with Suge too close behind, he opened the door, jumped in, slid across the seat, and came out the other side – with a .357 Magnum in hand! This he pointed directly at Suge's head, and then he cocked it. For obvious reasons, Suge stopped dead in his tracks and automatically raised his hands in the air, as if being robbed (or arrested!). The drama wasn't over, though, because Kim then snatched open the door of Suge's car and grabbed her 9 millimeter, aimed it at Dee, and screamed to Suge, "I got him! What do you want me to do?"

And into this disaster I now stepped. Really, it was like something out of a Quentin Tarentino film. Without thinking – since what thinking person would've done such a thing? – I propelled myself into the middle of the whole big mess, pleading with everybody to "Stop! Just stop!"...and ridiculously waving my cell phone in the air. My cell phone! No, I don't know what I intended to do with that phone, especially in a parking lot that was exploding with fear, embarrassment, confusion, anger, and obscenities, but it was the only weapon I had. And then, amazingly, it rang! What a bizarre moment for me to say, "Hello?" And how bizarre to hear Mike's voice on the other end, innocently asking, "So how did the meeting go?"

Well, what could I say? Everything had gone crazy, and every*body* had gone nuts, and it was broad daylight, and I was standing between two people who were holding loaded guns – and Mike wisely told me to hand the phone to Dee.

Mike: What's this all about?
Dee: This fat mutha is trippin.' He must think I'm a punk or somethin.' What you done did? Set me up?

Mike: What are you sayin,' man? Set you up for *what*? I sent you out there to watch him! What the hell am I gonna set you up for?

And this level of arguing and accusing went on for a while, until Mike had me give the phone to Suge.

Mike: What's really goin' on?
Suge: I thought this dude was disrespecting your lady at the meeting. [This "disrespect" was news to me, by the way, and the first of many lies I'd be hearing from Suge.] I was lookin' out for you and your best interests.
Mike: This is all bullshit, and if anything happens to my wife because of this crap, there'll be hell to pay for both of you!

And that was my first real taste of "business" in the macho world. That was how it was going to feel being a woman surrounded by testosterone. It was also the beginning of a severe and ugly rivalry between Suge and Dee, who wanted nothing less than to eliminate each other. It was my initiation into Suge's world of sabotage, bullying, and power. It was an education! And it was a clue to the unacceptable behaviors that had sentenced Suge and Dee, and Mike, to prison – and me to two years of waiting on those miserable courtroom benches.

"I was betrayed by [David] Kenner and Suge. I remember how Suge used to always say to me, 'We don't fatten no frogs for no snakes,' meaning that he didn't want undeserving individuals in the corporate world to benefit from our hard work. As it turned out, Suge ended up being both the frog and the snake."

– Michael Harris

THE NIGHTMARE AND THE DREAM

So let's think a little bit Godfather Entertainment and Death Row Records. We came together to create a major entertainment empire that would include recordings, movies, concerts, and merchandise, and at the beginning all of us had major parts to play.

- *David Kenner* was to defend Mike, Suge Knight, and others in their criminal cases, as well as to serve as entertainment attorney for the organization.
- *Suge Knight* supplied his considerable talent and was to act as everybody's manager.
- *Michael Harris* was to secure finances and invest the money through Kenner. At the time of his arrest, Mike had owned and operated several legitimate

businesses –businesses that included more than 150 employees on any given work day and that routinely paid local, state, and federal taxes. And, since he'd been a successful entrepreneur and Broadway producer by age twenty-six, he obviously had the financial and organizational skills that our company needed. Therefore, even from prison, the most natural thing in the world for him was to continue creating and building companies. [The arrangement actually wasn't quite as odd as it may sound, since Mike's federal conviction had been for drug violations, not money laundering.]

- *Andre "Dr. Dre" Young* was brought in because he was a multi-platinum producer and a hot commodity.
- *Michelle* was an artist whose debut LP had gone platinum and whose single went gold.
- *Doc Curry* was a hugely talented artist, also with a platinum debut album, but his career had been tragically limited because of an automobile accident that had severed his vocal chords. He remained with the company as a producer — a brilliant one.
- *P.B.L.. (Poor, Broke, and Lonely)* was an R&B group produced by Dre.
- Of course, I was Michael's connection to the outside world and a frequent liaison among all the other

Married to the Game

parties. And I held Michael, and our world, together. An inmate in a state prison cannot operate a business, so Michael was always a consultant to businesses that I'd run. We were partners. From the beginning of Godfather Entertainment, he was the negotiating-by-phone genius, and I was the day-to-day reality. My name was on all the paperwork!

With the new company taking shape, Suge was happy to be rid of some prior obligations, particularly Eric ("Eazy E") Wright and Ruthless Records, from whom he had obtained releases. On the other hand, there was some doubt as to the legality and validity of these releases, and there was even some question as to whether they might have been obtained under duress. And, in fact, David Kenner had to defend Suge and Death Row Records later on in a civil suit filed by Eazy E, Ruthless, and Jerry Heller. So things got off to an exciting but rocky start at Godfather Entertainment (and stayed that way!).

Even with a traditional law degree, David Kenner had a non-traditional background that was every bit as interesting as anybody else's in the corporation. While working with us, he had also been involved in several high-visibility criminal cases and had enjoyed a certain notoriety, especially on the East Coast.

- He defended ZZ Best's Barry Miko, who had created a hugely successful carpet cleaning business that he took public at a very young age – with the input of a bunch of mobsters.
- He represented "The Love Boat Killer," a notorious doctor who was indicted on federal murder charges for allegedly throwing his wife overboard in international waters but who had originally claimed that she'd been abducted by Israeli soldiers.
- He was the attorney for a lead defendant in "The Cotton Club Murder."

Despite David's fame, or infamy, despite the fact that I once trusted him and confided in him, despite how he shamelessly took advantage of me...in his own way he helped me develop the much more realistic *dis*trust that I feel for lawyers today. Because of my dedication to my husband and because of all the conversations that I had with lawyers on his behalf, I think I can now be considered something of an expert on the legal profession and on individuals like David Kenner. In terms of the prison population, lawyers are the true gatekeepers. They make deals with the government, often behind their clients' backs. Without visible remorse, they frequently utilize the attorney/client privilege as a means of attaining information that can then be turned over to the other side. They're capable of playing with their clients' lives as if every case were a poker game and every defendant had a dollar value – which I suppose is true! And because the clients are so totally dependent on their attorneys, they become slaves to the situation. I'm not fond of lawyers.

Regardless, I'll spare you most of the tiresome legal and financial details that all but made the government an equal partner in the birth of our entertainment firm. Suffice it to say that, at my husband's request, David Kenner functioned outside prison walls to distribute monies for the professional activities, and the courtroom defense, of Ruthless Records, Andre "Dr. Dre" Young, Calvin "Snoop Dogg" Broadus, and Marion "Suge" Knight – until Interscope assumed Kenner's responsibilities later in the game.

"One thing I will say is that I was never paid for the legal work I did for Mr. Harris. I am sincerely disappointed by Mr. Harris' attitude."

– Attorney David Kenner

LOW PROFILE

I always walked quietly around the industry, even when I was new and didn't know anything. Even when I still had a great desire to believe everything I heard and to trust everybody I met, I somehow knew that there were shady things going on, and I wasn't a shady person. I had hunches about folks whose money was questionable. I realized that there were liars in the business. I watched and learned, and soon I saw that things weren't going the right way. My hard work and good intentions were a big joke to far too many people. What was on the surface – in other words, what the world saw – was much, much smaller than the reality underneath.

Now, it took me a while to realize that nobody had my back. Nobody! People could count on *me,* but at the end of every crisis I was always alone. I had to solve my own dilemmas and plan my own professional recoveries. I had to grow strong.

Despite my marriage to Michael Harris, I am my own woman. I'm capable of making decisions independently, and in my business dealings I've remained separate from the drama and the dark side of all that a prison life represents. My money has come from *my efforts.* I've had to tell people, "You're not doing business with Michael. I don't even have a parking ticket. I've done nothing wrong." But every day has been a huge up-hill battle.

I can remember reading and hearing about the children of movie stars or famous athletes or other very, very rich parents. Each of them has said, "I've succeeded in spite of my father's money" or "I've made it in spite of my mother's fame." Every one of them has considered his family name to be a handicap even while admitting that that same name has presented him with the kinds of opportunities that most "ordinary" people will never enjoy.

Well, I understand those folks! Being married to Michael Harris, knowing famous people, and having my name associated with Death Row Records has probably opened hundreds of doors for me. But it has also slammed many others in my face. There's still a stigma attached to prisoners, rappers, and street thugs of all types, especially in the mainstream world. And that's why, even though I've known some of those notorious people, gotten along well with some of them, done business with a long list of them, and married one of them, I'm still my own person. When you talk with me, you're not talking to a committee.

I just want you to know that I *can* distinguish myself from my marriage.

WOMEN!

First there was Kim, the "Paradise" who had offered to get rid of Dee for Suge Knight. Compared to her, Michelle was just a voice, although my early impressions of her were strange.

I already knew that Michelle's career was a family affair, *literally* – an NWA family affair. Dr. Dre was her boyfriend and the father of her son, Eazy E was her producer, and of course Jerry Heller was her manager. Lots of families are dysfunctional beneath the surface, though, and theirs was no exception. Despite their enormous success in the industry, neither Michelle nor Dre knew anything about business, and I was shocked to realize that they were no more than puppets for Jerry Heller's puppet show. Even after Suge grabbed control of NWA from Jerry, all the attitude and confidence that Michelle and Dre projected to the public in their singing and rapping were nonexistent at the conference table. Amazing as the thought seems, they basically did as they were told. Meanwhile, Michelle's second album, which was already long overdue, slipped into the category known as "indefinitely on hold" as brighter stars such as Mary J. Blige sailed past her.

All of a sudden everyone's focus was on Mary. Of all the comers, she was quickly crowned "The Queen of Hip-Hop Soul," and she probably deserved the title. She was a huge asset to our company, and I had and have tremendous respect for her as an artist and a woman. I have to admit, though, that I often felt eclipsed by her very presence – and I'm not a jealous woman. But her enormous success, and the real confidence that came with it, seemed to remind me that my own dream of becoming a singer was fading. As Michael's wife, my talent for *business* was needed, and that was what consumed my energies and my time. Still, I couldn't help wondering whether Mary was singing about her own experiences, as presented to the public, or whether she was just another product, a *concept* of a "ghetto queen."

I didn't merely wonder about Veronica, though: I worried. Veronica Davis is in her thirties, an actress and model of German/African descent who looks European. Although she had a degree in journalism, she owned several businesses, including a massage parlor that did house calls. She's stunning and obviously tempting.

Mike first met her at one of a series of pool parties hosted by Earvin "Magic" Johnson, who would offer five thousand dollars to the winner of a swimsuit competition. This "entertainment" called for the women to dance around the pool, dive off the board, and then be judged for their figures and their swim wear. Some of the contenders would do outrageous things to win, including removing their suits, but Veronica didn't need any help. She simply bounced on the diving board a few times and allowed her ample breasts to drive the men crazy.

Mike and I always discussed everything, *everything*, so I know that he was taken with Veronica that night. And even though it was assumed that Magic would always claim the winner at the end of the evening, on that occasion Mike broke with tradition and persuaded Veronica and her entourage to caravan all the way from Bel Air to his mansion in Encino instead. Magic was not happy.

After that passionate beginning, Mike and Veronica's relationship escalated dramatically, and for a while he contemplated marrying her. Once he and I had gotten married, in fact, she still professed herself eternally devoted to him. And I'm not the jealous type, but – yes, she's the exception to my rule. She even showed her support of Mike by attending one of his trials with some of her equally gorgeous, glamorous friends, who caused such an uproar with their seductive behavior that the prosecutor pleaded with the judge to have them leave the premises, and he did!

Of course, Veronica was a distraction wherever she went. Even David Kenner, whose marriage was on the rocks, fell for her and begged Mike to set him up with her. I suppose we could say that Mike used Veronica to "keep David's spirits up." However, Mike's generosity came back to haunt him. When Suge noticed that David had fallen in love with Veronica but was completely insecure about her lingering feelings for Mike, he took advantage of this love triangle and convinced David that Veronica would desert him for Mike the minute Mike gained his freedom from prison. After that little bit of soap-opera psychology, David lost interest in Mike's defense, Mike languished in prison, and Suge seized control of the corporation – which he then, ironically, tried to maintain from behind bars.

"You have to realize what kind of guy this is. Michael Harris makes things up to try to get out of jail. What he wanted from me was to make a record for his wife. In exchange, he offered me the group The Geto Boys. There were two big problems with that. One, he didn't own The Geto Boys. And two, she couldn't sing."

– Suge Knight

AND ONE WOMAN IN PARTICULAR

The longest and most involved of all my Girl Stories, though, features a seemingly sweet young thing named Jamie Alexander, who would eventually teach me all I'd ever need to know about wolves in sheep's clothing.

I met Jamie at the creation of Death Row Records, and I immediately (and with much inaccuracy, I admit) characterized her as intelligent and attractive, with a lovely disposition. And, since I lived such an odd, theatrical life, maybe I simply needed a friend I could count on – someone without all the underhandedness and ulterior motives associated with most of the folks I then knew. She'd been hired by Suge as a receptionist for the studio switchboard; but, as Jamie herself would tell me, she'd also been one of his girlfriends, even though his *public* relationship at the time was with Kim – yes, the same Kim from the parking-lot "battle," the passive-aggressive Kim whose aggressive side would often overcome the passive in outbursts of violent behavior.

For instance, it wasn't at all unusual for Kim to throw gale-force temper tantrums and to berate or physically attack the young rappers and producers who frequented the studio. However, these people were so terrified of Suge's potential for wrath and retaliation that they tended to humor Kim or give in to her irrational demands. Anything was preferable to dealing with Suge!

Of course, this was already an intense and exciting chapter in our lives. Dr. Dre, Warren G, D.O.C., Snoop Dogg, Tha Dog Pound, Jewell Payton, Glove, Rage, DJ Unknown, the rapper Black, the producer Chocolate – these and many other industry figures were virtually *living* at the studio, and it was a madhouse! In many ways the time, the place, the passion, and the energy reminded me of a very young Motown, back when it was headquartered in somebody's small, unpretentious house in Detroit.

Much of the melodrama of Godfather Entertainment originated with Suge and Kim, naturally, and I somehow became the only person she'd confide in when she was in one of her rages and he wasn't around. Luckily for me, she *was* capable of calming down and even being pleasant sometimes. It amazed me, though, that Jamie was bold enough and rash enough to have an affair with Suge while seeming to be Kim's "friend" because, even though the P.R. people referred to Kim as "Paradise," "*Dynamite*" might've been a more accurate nickname!

And too this whole behind-Kim's-back thing should've been a warning to me about Jamie's lack of character. Instead, I managed to feel sorry for her because Suge mistreated her, which he undeniably did. Public humiliation was one of his favorite hobbies, as was his tendency to use "his" women for sex toys. In Jamie's particular situation, he also opted not to compensate her fairly for the outstanding job she was doing for the company, and as a result he was able to control her and dominate her life: she was broke *and* financially dependent specifically on him.

Sometimes, then – soft touch that I've always been – I would give her money to tide her over. And I'd plead with her to *do* something: "Don't you have any respect for yourself, Jamie? Why do you let him treat you like this?" I have to say, though, that her answers never completely satisfied me. During one of our many repetitive conversations about the same old subject, I came to the conclusion that Jamie was attracted by dangerous, dogmatic men, with the emphasis on the "dog." And many, many women within and around the rap industry shared her addiction.

Not so with me, though. In fact, Mike and I were rapidly deciding that I needed to be spending less time at the studio. The atmosphere at Death Row had always been hectic and volatile, thanks to all the conflicting personalities, egos, and temperaments hanging around the premises, and now it was violent as well. Guns were being fired *inside* the building. People were getting beaten up! For my own physical safety, we determined that I needed to get some physical distance from the place. And so I lost contact with Jamie for a couple of years.

When our paths finally crossed again, she told me that she'd parted company with Suge and was living with her parents so that they could help care for her young daughter when her job took her on the road. I told her that I'd just created a new label, Lifestyle Records, and also that I'd bought a house in Lancaster, California, in order to be closer to my husband. Since the new home had five bedrooms, a pool, and a tennis court, I felt justified in encouraging Jamie and her little girl to spend some time with me.

Unfortunately, this invitation was yet another instance of what happens when I drop my guard. You see, I had been so terribly lonely without Mike that the thought of being around a friend, a kindred spirit, was a source of great happiness for me. I even went beyond the invitation to visit and, with Mike's blessing, asked the two of them to move in with me. Everything would be perfect! Jamie could even become my paid assistant. It was one of those rare and obvious win-win situations.

And, at first, everything was terrific. Jamie and I talked girl talk, played tennis, and ate – *a lot*. Since I'm from Texas, I love cooking and entertaining Texas-style, and Texas-style means huge, tasty feasts enthusiastically prepared for appreciative folks with hearty appetites. And my new kitchen was so enormous and spectacular that all of us could stretch out and have fun in it.

Nevertheless, after about five months, Jamie disappeared again – this time to San Francisco. She definitely left her imprint on my life, though, because, immediately after her departure, a lot of very strange people began to show up on my doorstep, and a lot of ominous things began to happen. Now, whether Suge had traced one of her phone calls from my house (since obviously her separation from him hadn't been complete), or whether she'd irresponsibly *given* him my new address and extremely private phone number, I don't know. But I can assure you that it wasn't paranoia alone that persuaded me to hire a twenty-four-hours-a-day security patrol!

A year later, I ran into Jamie yet again. Her explanation for the vanishing act? "I had gotten myself involved in something really dangerous before I moved in with you. It was catching up with me, so I left in order to keep you from danger." Why she couldn't have shared this information with me earlier, who knows? And whatever happened to her daughter and her parents during these cloak-and-dagger times, she neglected to mention.

And *still* I tried to rescue her. Call me stupid or, if you want to be kind, naive; either way, I actually invited Jamie to share my new place in L.A. I wanted to help her. I was always lonely. I missed having girlfriends to talk to in the cut-throat, male-dominated world of rap music. Whatever! I repeated my poor decision from a year and a half earlier, and again I paid a heavy price for a lousy judgment call.

Seeking a more dependable security system (largely because of Jamie herself, of course), I had left the big house in Lancaster and moved into a condominium on

Wilshire Boulevard, in Westwood. At the same time, and as my special brand of bad luck would have it, Tupac Shakur, Suge Knight, and their guys had *also* purchased a condo...exactly two doors down from mine! Since they used their place only once in a while, though, to crash in, they weren't even aware of my presence – that is, until Jamie volunteered the information. Evidently, that was her way of keeping me from danger!

And my unsettled life continued. Having retreated from my house, I also found myself closing down Lifestyle Records, thanks to some turmoil and fall-out from Warner Brothers and Maverick (which, incidentally, was Madonna's label). Because of a heated anti-rap campaign waged by William Bennett, Bob Dole, and African-American political activist DeLores Tucker (talk about strange bedfellows!), Lifestyle had been pushed and shoved into bankruptcy.

So now I was in the process of forming yet another corporation – New Image Entertainment. I just desperately wanted, needed, and envisioned a fresh start. Besides, it was crucial to me that Mike and I separate ourselves from Suge Knight's street style of doing business. Hiring Jamie once more to serve as my executive assistant, I threw myself into creating a powerful, respected entertainment company that would be completely run by women – an innovation! However, Jamie was, as ever, full of surprises, and I guess I was a very slow learner. *Very* slow.

And what *she* was was bisexual. Now, I don't care about any of that; and, as a matter of fact, as soon as I heard the rumors about Jamie, I made it a point to speak with her very frankly. I said, "If it's true, my feeling is that what a person does is her business as long as she doesn't come at me twisted." And I meant it! But Jamie denied the whole thing – and, besides, I was still priding myself on being a good judge of people. (Hard to believe! I know! I know!) But here was somebody I'd known a rather long time – somebody I'd even had to share a bed with once or twice – and she'd never given me the smallest hint that she was into women. On the other hand, I hadn't been *looking* for hints. But time would eventually prove even to someone as trusting as me that Jamie was a totally scandalous set-up artist and one of the most obvious freaks around.

So who figured her out? Mike. Yes, even from behind prison walls he was perceptive enough to discover the real deal. He'd never seen Jamie, *but* he used to spend long stretches of time on the phone with her while she took dictation from him, *and* he's always had a talent for uncovering the most amazingly personal secrets about folks, *and* – she confided in him. As simple as that.

Have you ever seen the great old Bette Davis movie "All about Eve"? Well, Jamie was a natural for the Anne Baxter part. Evidently she'd fallen in love with Mike's mind – and my lifestyle! – and she was determined to take my place. I don't know exactly how Mike managed to draw all the details out of her, including the part about how she wanted to "have" me, but it's good that she didn't get around to sharing all the specifics with *me*. Then too, I can't imagine how she planned to seduce me *and* replace me, so let me just be grateful that I don't have a mind like hers. What a mess!

Suddenly, but at long last, it became quite clear to me that I had invited a monster into my life – and it was equally clear that I had to get her *out*! Even though I've lived for years at the very center of the rap industry, I don't thrive on deception, tension, craziness, or destructiveness. I don't seek out personal gratification, greed, twisted pleasure, or extreme ego. No – perhaps surprisingly, there's a limit to what I can co-exist with, and I could no longer co-exist with Jamie. I could pray for her, and I did, but God had given her choices, including the choice to do something good with her life, and somehow she'd decided to follow a different path. I was through trying.

"Believe it or not, my secret to remaining a good person in the midst of all bad things is always to put God first and surrender myself to Him. That is how I maintain."

– My pledge to God

AN UNHOLY WAR

Throughout our marriage, Michael Harris and I struggled with conspiracies and fought off attacks from some strange and unexpected sources, and at one point we found ourselves targeted by the Jewish Defense League *and* the Nation of Islam! Now, *that* was an uncomfortable place.

A Muslim brother named Shahied, who had been a stone-cold street hustler and notorious jacker before his conversion, took it upon himself (or so he said) to do something about the "immorality" of Death Row Records and the music we were producing. In reality, what Shahied wanted was a worldly piece of the action. He was good too – very convincing – and he played some fascinating mind games with the legal eagles behind Priority Distribution, Ruthless Records, and their former artist Ice Cube. His new spirituality had done nothing to erase Shahied's street smarts!

What Ice Cube had done was to release an album that depicted his Jewish ex-manager, Mike Klein, in a disrespectful way, or at least in a way that was *perceived* to be disrespectful to Klein and to the Jewish community as a whole. Behind all the self-righteous noise, though, Klein was secretly cooperating with Shahied in a scheme to benefit them both. If you can believe this:

- Klein's job was to announce publicly that the JDL was putting a hit out on Ice Cube.
- Shahied, supposedly under the auspices of the Muslim community, would offer Cube protection from the JDL.
- At the same time, Shahied would attempt to become Ice Cube's manager while also (and almost as an afterthought) converting him to Islam!

How slick can a couple of "religious" hypocrites be? Well, they weren't nearly so slick as Suge Knight and David Kenner. And, even from prison, Mike Harris was not in the habit of being anybody's fool.

There was going to be a summit meeting between Suge and Shahied. With twenty of his guys, Shahied

Married to the Game

planned to demonstrate the kind of protection he was offering to Ice Cube. But in a beautifully choreographed move, Mike had arranged to telephone Suge during the meeting. So, on cue, Suge handed the phone to Shahied; and then – surprising even Suge – fifteen of Mike's guys filed into the room while Mike pointedly informed Shahied that, "As you can see, we have no need for your services. This is *my* bread and butter! Back off!"

What happened after this little episode was that Shahied was expelled from his mosque for attempting to use the Muslim community as a front for illegal activities. And Mike Klein, who continued struggling for control of Ruthless Records through a tiresome string of legal ploys and publicity tricks, gained nothing for his questionable efforts. However, there was a sad footnote to the whole sorry thing.

Eazy E, who by then was dying of AIDS, signed over Ruthless Records to his wife, Tamika Wright. Yet immediately after his death, Mike Klein again surfaced, this time for the purpose of contesting Eazy's right of ownership and his right to leave the company to Tamika. Realistically speaking, I have to admit that Ruthless – with talent such as NWA, Bone, Thugs & Harmony, and M.C. Ren on the payroll – was financially worth fighting for! But justice prevailed, and the case was settled in Tamika Wright's favor.

Shahied and Klein taught me a lesson, though: they taught me that, sometimes, "religion" isn't very religious.

"You and Suge and I are partners, Mike. We're all partners."

– David Kenner

HOW IT WORKS

One week, a major label signs you. The next week, it shifts you to another major label. The week after that, you're dropped entirely. And the whole ugly process can make you really, really dizzy.

CHECKMATE

In every corner, every angle, every chapter of my story there's Suge Knight, as I'm sure you've noticed. Our relationship with him has been bad, if not impossible, and it was deteriorating further during the time that I moved back to L.A. and began working on the New Image project.

I had just called Jimmy Iovine at Interscope to inform — or remind — him that our original company, Godfather Entertainment, owned fifty percent of Death Row Records. I further informed him that Mike and I were preparing to file a lawsuit against Death Row and Interscope (a suit that we fully expected to win, if things went that far).

Jimmy's response was incredulous: "Why are you suing us? We're only Death Row's *distributor*! You need to speak to Suge and Kenner and get straight on what my company's percentage of Death Row really is!"

I should tell you that I don't like being underestimated. In fact, I knew quite well that this was a bad time for Jimmy, Interscope, and Ted Fields because they had just been dropped by Atlantic/WEA. Also, they were in the middle of signing a deal with MCA, Polygram, or EMI for a fifty-percent partnership and distribution rights. Now, all of this major activity was taking place when Interscope's estimated value was a staggering $500 million, and Death Row was bringing in half of its profits. Half! Death Row was worth $250 million, and Godfather's share was $125 million! Yes, I was completely aware of how unpopular our lawsuit would be with these people.

So, even though my stomach was in an uproar during my conversation with Jimmy, all he heard in my *voice* was icy composure. After all, a lot was riding on the call I'd just made! I knew I was opening Pandora's box, but my course was set. Mike was depending on me, and I was ready. I make it a point in business always to be ready. And I make it a point in life always to be dependable.

Anyway, I coolly suggested that Jimmy get back to me after he'd touched base with Kenner and Suge – and, sure enough, within a couple of minutes my phone rang! It was Suge, who obviously had me on the loudspeaker even while trying to convince me otherwise, and he was using those artificially casual telephone manners that folks lapse into whenever they're trying to impress somebody: "Hey, Lyd! What's goin' on?"

I just cut him short, though, and got down to business. "You *know* what's going on, so let's just call a timeout from all these damn games you've been playing. We want our money, and we want it now."

Well, Suge blew his cool at this ultimatum! He was angry, and he was loud! I don't think he'd expected such brass from me. However, I still had work to do, so I clicked over to the other phone to see if Mike was on the line to David Kenner's office, and of course he was – because we were a team, and because even a prison wall couldn't separate us or keep our minds from working together. So after telling him that Suge was on the phone, talking crazy and threatening me, I got back on the line with Suge and encouraged him to call Mike and verbally attack him the same way he'd attacked me. And Suge did it! He actually threatened and harassed Michael Harris! Of course, he didn't win the discussion.

It was probably this incident, by the way, that gave birth to the false rumor that Suge Knight had slapped me, which he never did. Oh, he assaulted me, but only with words – and I was not impressed.

"I don't want to talk to Mike. Mike's a rat. David Kenner told me Mike's a rat."

– Suge Knight

PSYCHO/ANALYZING

It must've gone something like this: he saw the name "Lifestyle," looked at our label, felt the old greed and jealousy waking up again inside his head, got scared silly that we might soon be enjoying better treatment from Interscope than Death Row was, panicked, and decided to ruin my life or die trying. But that's what insecure people do, don't they?

You know who I'm talking about.

WHAT THE PAPERS SAY

It always amazes me to hear and see what the media and others will project as the truth about me, about Michael, about our business dealings, and about our married life. Sometimes I think I must be having a science-fiction hallucination when I remember some of the "facts" that have been connected to us.

My husband initiated the creation of Death Row Records in 1991 when he introduced David Kenner, who was his lawyer, to Suge Knight, a one-time football player who aspired to become a music entrepreneur and who happened to have access to a Hollywood recording studio. Talk to Kenner or Knight today about Death Row, however, and they seem to have forgotten much of the significance of Michael's involvement at the outset.

Within months of that early meeting, Michael had put up 1.5 million dollars of his own money for a half stake in Godfather Entertainment. Now, one of the main reasons that Michael invested so much money was that Suge Knight promised him Andre "Dr. Dre" Young as producer; and almost immediately the group began production on Dre's "Chronic" album, which was to be Death Row's debut release. Suge has forgotten some of that attachment too, even though he visited Michael in prison at least a couple of dozen times during the next year and a half. At the company's grand-opening party in 1992, he was even *videotaped paying tribute to Michael* – though in later interviews he strongly suggested that this same Michael was a liar and a rat.

Still, it was Suge and Dr. Dre who went behind Michael's back to cut a deal with Interscope, which then released "Chronic" and a string of other multimillion-dollar hits. And now Suge claims that it wasn't Michael who financed the creation of Death Row Records. Instead, he's decided that the label got off the ground because Sony, Interscope, and Time Warner provided millions of dollars for the project. I suppose I should pity him for his astounding loss of memory – though not for his ability to make money: between 1993 and 1997, Death Row's music earned more than 300 million dollars in retail sales. Does Michael know that he was obscenely betrayed? Oh, yes.

Suge Knight went to prison for violating his probation (he had been convicted on an assault charge), and he seemed to find time while there to accuse my husband of cutting deals with the government. As Mike has always insisted, though, and as I can obviously verify, all of his documents were subpoenaed. He never made a deal, and he never involved anyone else in his legal problems. He was man enough to place the burden on his own back, and he's carried it there, with help from me – since 1988.

And then how about the Rap-a-Lot rumors? In 1987, with a handshake and two hundred thousand dollars, Mike agreed to help his "friend" James "Li'l J" Smith create the Rap-a-Lot label. Within almost no time, of course, Li'l J forgot all about Mike's help and denied that there'd ever been an understanding at all. He also disagreed – loudly – with Mike over ownership of Dana Dane's music. Then, following in Suge Knight's footsteps, he signed a multimillion-dollar distribution pact with Virgin Records in 1995, separating Mike from Rap-a-Lot very effectively. And in his strange version of what had actually happened, he then decided that he'd financed Rap-a-Lot with his own money. Such crazy hindsight fascinates me.

And the media...

My husband has always admitted that for several years he dealt drugs and made tremendous money in the process. However, the courts and the media continue to say in addition that he attempted to murder one of his own employees who was also a distant relative. *That* didn't happen.

And it's an exaggeration to report, as all the media did, that Michael was the central witness in a federal racketeering investigation of Death Row Records. Certainly he was involved with the creation and the early days of Death Row, even from behind bars, but why single him out as a key figure in the federal probe? Isn't it obvious that other people began removing him from the company almost as soon as they removed him from his money? As recently as June, 2004, a media giant as respected as the *Los Angeles Business Journal* referred to Death Row Records as Suge Knight's record label!

Of all the terrible things that have happened to our family, though, one of the worst was the low moment in 1996 when my husband became mysteriously ill and was coerced into signing a settlement with Interscope that released all claims to Death Row Records in return for three hundred thousand dollars – and I wasn't there to fend off the attack. Now, would a well man accept a $300,000 settlement for a $1.5 million investment? Would anyone accept twenty cents on the dollar? And yet the Los Angeles Superior Court dismissed our claim even while admitting that Death Row (now calling itself Tha Row) had violated certain procedures in its dealings with us.

Yes, and "Tha Row" had committed fraud, conspiracy, unfair business practices, and defamation of character – for years!

"I am not afraid of the truth. But I am truly disturbed by these insinuations that I am some kind of a rat. I am not a rat. If I was a rat, I could have been home free ten years ago. "

– Michael Harris

PLAY THE GAME, AND THE GAME PLAYS YOU

No matter what you read in the papers or see on BET, there used to be more than one "Dre," and now I want you to hear about the *other* one – Andre Harris.

Despite his last name, he wasn't related to Mike except for looking up to him as a father figure. They had known each other early on, and Dre re-entered the picture after Mike went to prison. He'd heard on the streets that Suge and Mike were partners in Death Row Records, and he wanted in. Mike (ever loyal to the old days) was open to this suggestion, but the only reason Suge went along with it must've been because he smelled an opportunity to beat Dre out of something. I mean, if Suge had twenty million dollars and you had a hundred dollars, he'd want your hundred! I've never met a greedier person. I have to say, though, that Mike tried to protect Dre by warning Suge not to underestimate him just because he looked like a nerd. He was actually a very dangerous nerd. Mike instructed Suge to leave Dre's little piece of change alone!

So Dre was a partner in Lifestyle Records & Productions, basically becoming our A&R rep and using his street savvy to attract some new and talented rappers and producers (Battlecat, Befee, Black Czar) to the company. Finally there was someone by my side that I could trust to protect our interests! Dre assisted me in deals involving Interscope, Maverick, East/West Records, and other huge names, as well as in taking over the management of P.B.L. – a change that infuriated Suge!

To this day I believe that Dre had everything he needed to become an A-list music executive, and I wish we could've put him in the driver's seat for our corporation. However, he could never shake his insatiable need for the window dressing, the desire to be seen, to be perceived as a big shot. And he was full of rage inside. Naturally, this part of Dre's character troubled Mike and me because it seemed so reminiscent of Suge. Both of them craved the lifestyle that Mike was determined to leave behind – and together they were explosive!

There's always some history that explains why people are the way they are, and a major contributor to all of Dre's problems was his lack of a real family. He never even knew his father's name. But he admired my husband so much that he changed his own last name to Harris, illustrating the love, respect, and loyalty that he felt for Mike (and blowing a gasket in Suge's ugly mood). And...just maybe Dre was also using the name-change gesture as something of a power play because he knew that it was the kind of thing Suge would've done.

Regardless, after that dramatic act, Suge never again missed an opportunity to undermine Dre's character to Mike, and the rivalry between the two got so intense that Dre actually contemplated killing Suge, David Kenner, and L'il J! Mike was constantly cooling him down then, reminding him that "there are other ways to resolve these matters." And, luckily, Mike the father figure was able time and again to persuade Dre to back away from a situation.

Even Mike couldn't give Dre self-control and patience, though, and eventually our worst fears were realized when we lost him forever. It was such a sad and stupid thing, and deadly: Dre had set up a million-dollar drug deal, with the intention of robbing the dealers. The plan went haywire, though, and it played out like another really bad movie when Dre and his partner murdered the two dealers and were leaving the scene of their crime with the money when they themselves were shot from the back and killed. What a terrible waste – literally.

Through the years I've constantly been asked why Mike allowed Suge Knight, David Kenner, L'il J, and others to get away with so much garbage for so long. Well, he didn't plan things this way. Because of his incarceration, Mike's power has repeatedly been tested and challenged by the people closest to him, and many times he's been able to keep the lid on things. But his special circumstances have also controlled *him*.

Believe me, he hasn't enjoyed being betrayed, and it was definitely within his realm of possibility to handle Suge, Kenner, and L'il J the old-fashioned way. After all, he knows people who know people. But Mike has always preferred to use his mind, his obvious intelligence, in something very much like a life-sized game of chess. And he has a major talent for staying focused on the big picture. He has plans. He has a design for a towering new entertainment empire. Let those guys be defeated by their own greed and hatred: he's the only one armed for a battle of wits.

But another thing about Suge and Li'l J: they have the same contempt and disregard for women that too many rappers are known for. Or maybe it's partly fear? They want their women barefoot and pregnant, or displayed like trophies to bolster their own images. Just consider how little they'd appreciate somebody like me!

Mike was different, of course. He was always capable of seeing women in the light of their highest potential, and he always encouraged them to fulfill that potential. Certainly he did it with me.

Now, I don't begin to know how he managed to see in me the professional capabilities that I didn't realize I had. During his incarceration, though, he called on me again and again to execute moves that I never would've forecast for myself – and I would win! In my own heart I've always suspected that I've been able to accomplish so much success because I don't do things for me alone, but also for Mike, for my parents and my brother, and for Lydasia. And too I often gained strength from the realization that, even from behind prison bars, Mike had my back. If anyone attempted to disrespect me or minimize me solely because I was a woman, Mike and his guys would quickly instruct that man in the error of his ways.

The power that I've had at my disposal always outraged Suge Knight and others like him. Because my loyalty to Mike was unquestionable, I was absolutely unapproachable. The terrifying result of my connection to Mike, though, was that our enemies finally realized that the only way to hurt him, the only way to shut him down, was to kill me, and many, many people were willing to carry out that intent. So my life has been infiltrated by true danger and death threats that I still have to cope with.

And yet the danger and the threats are a burden I can bear because I don't have to bear them alone. Even with the rest of the world going crazy, I'm sustained by the realization that I'm strong, and God is with me. My life and my family's happiness, safety, and freedom mean much more to me than Death Row Records, Rap-a-Lot, or making another deal. We're all right!

"Mike Harris is a pathological lying snitch. I guess he must be working with the feds trying to bring down Black-owned companies."

– James "L'il J" Smith

WHAT YOU DON'T UNDERSTAND

When Mike was a free man, he of course ran some successful businesses, but he also owned several gorgeous custom-built homes in breathtaking environments, and those were the places where he entertained his lady friends, including me. Every time we made love on his incredible marble bed, it seemed as though we were the only two people on the planet.

And he always made me feel as if I were his queen. One of his companies was a limo service, and the drivers also treated me royally. Whenever I traveled from Texas to visit him in Los Angeles, Mike would take me to the most exclusive clubs and restaurants and on romantic limousine rides along the magnificent Pacific Coast Highway. It was a dream! And yet I always realized that, even though I treasured all of his efforts and his generosity, it was the *man* I'd fallen in love with, not the lifestyle. And in a strange way I almost appreciate these later years of hardships and challenges because these times are real, and those, perhaps, weren't.

As I hinted at earlier, California was one of ten states that allowed their prisoners to have 36- to 48-hour unsupervised overnight family visits every 45 or 60 days. This was a merciful policy designed to preserve the family bond, and I was incredibly grateful for it, especially because it brought us our little girl.

I know it's an odd thing for me to say, especially since my time with Mike when he was still free was incomparably glamorous, extravagant, and thrilling, but our most precious moments together were during those conjugal visits. Lancaster State Prison provided a two-bedroom log cabin, plain but clean and cozy, and on one of my visits with Mike that cabin became a chalet in the French Alps when we were blessed with a beautiful. driving snowfall.

Since the prison permitted families to bring in groceries from the outside, the Texas girl in me would always cook a roomful of food for my husband. Then we'd simply forget the world, and I would at last feel safe. And of course we'd make love all day and all night!

So even if I sound trite saying so, this is the truth: experiences like those – a couple of days in a simple cabin, eating homemade food and just being together – helped me understand and fully appreciate the basics of life, things like love, trust, and commitment. That's why nothing, not even a very long prison separation, ever caused me to turn my back on my husband or our wedding vows.

In the beginning, I made a conscious decision to enter into and remain in a relationship with Mike. Later I was stunned to see that being his woman would be difficult – and dangerous! But the difficulties and the dangers never shook my resolve to remain with him, and that's because I fell in love with him the first moment I saw his face – and because I'm a very, very loyal woman. In case you hadn't already noticed, let me admit now that I've spent a lot of years thinking with my heart.

There's very little that I don't know about devotion.

"For richer or poorer, in sickness and in health, through good times and bad, until death do us part, I will love and cherish you and honor this vow."

– My pledge to my husband

THE FEDERAL PROBE

I won't pretend that the rap business has had a peaceful history, and it probably won't surprise you to learn that, following the violent deaths of Biggie Smalls and Tupac Shakur, federal agents showed up *with subpoenas* at Godfather Entertainment's front door. Believe me, their visit was unpleasant and definitely unwelcome because it was more than a standard law-enforcement reaction to some shocking national events. In fact, it was the culmination of a media smear campaign that had RICO (the Feds' Racketeer-Influenced and Corrupt Organizations department) stamped all over it. It also had nothing to do with us.

I can assure you – and who would know better than me? – that our money dealings have always been straight-up. With me at the desk, Godfather paid its taxes and kept accurate records and did whatever our lawyers told us to do. But those subpoenas were just the latest in a lengthy, heavy-handed government effort to control the entire urban music industry. It's been obvious to me that some people in high places cannot adjust to the reality of having "urban" (in other words, African-American) entrepreneurs making big money, legitimately, as a result of the rap enterprise. Bob Dole, William Bennett, and DeLores Tucker may have ranted and raved about what a bad influence the music itself was, but we knew that the *intent* of their attack went far beyond what they would've been willing to admit. They had a desire to close us down and keep us closed, and we knew it, so we were determined not to give them any ammunition: we kept everything honest, legal, and above reproach. Black-owned businesses always have to try harder than anybody else. That's our reality!

Besides, this wasn't the first time that Mike had been targeted in a major federal campaign. A decade earlier — "coincidentally" – William Bennett had labeled Mike a national drug kingpin and utilized the ensuing headlines to further his own political agenda. But as for the probe...

Once Godfather's and Lifestyle's financial records had been subpoenaed, right away I had to hire attorneys and accountants for an FBI/IRS audit. It's a good thing I've always been precise, forthright, and legitimate in all my business dealings! So of course the audit turned up no irregularities. So of course the Feds extended their harassment to every company and every executive I was doing business with. And when *that* ploy didn't work, they began to lean on record-industry people, heavily. And still their questioning failed to turn up any discrepancies.

However, the aggressiveness of the federal campaign was plenty to create a "blackball" situation, and slowly we found ourselves being frozen out. Thank God, though – some companies in the industry refused to be bullied and actually continued doing business with us.

Let me be quick to say, on the other hand, that it wasn't just federal agencies and industry outsiders that attempted to overthrow us. In fact, I filed, on behalf of Godfather Entertainment, a lawsuit against Death Row Records, Interscope Records, James "Li'l J" (Rap-a-Lot Records) Smith, Suge Knight, and David Kenner – for defamation of character *and* to reclaim ownership of our percentage of Death Row and Rap-a-Lot. This I did, not simply for the money, which was obviously a huge amount, or for damages, but as a way of forcing *all* parties to place their cards on the table. Anyway, why not share some of the attention that Mike and I were always getting from the FBI and the IRS?

" In late 1991, Michael Harris, Suge Knight, and David Kenner met at the Metropolitan Detention Center in Los Angeles to form a company which came to be known as Death Row Records. The focus of my involvement was to assist David Kenner and Suge Knight on behalf of my husband's fifty-percent interest in this venture. Because Michael was in prison, he could not operate or participate in the business. For that reason, I was chosen to be an owner and to manage the Harris' share. Suge Knight and I each would own fifty percent of the business." [Wasserman, Comden, Casselman & Pearson, L.L.P., Tarzana, California]

– Plaintiff's application

BRINGING COLOR TO THE GREAT WHITE WAY

In 1988 and 1989, my husband Michael spent his last eighteen months of freedom producing a successful Broadway play through his theatrical company, Y Not Productions. "Checkmates" was a four-character drama that provided the kinds of showy, significant stage roles that had rarely been available for black actors and actresses. Mike sensed that a change was overdue in the American theater, and he wanted to be that change.

"Checkmate" was an ideal vehicle for the wonderful Denzel Washington, who performed in it on Broadway (and in Los Angeles) and whose career gained tremendous credibility from the experience. "Checkmate" also proved crucial for Vanessa Williams, who'd been unable to get hired for a straight acting job until then. I absolutely believe that she learned to act during the run of this show, in a role which drew from her the grace, subtlety, and self-confidence that her audiences can now take for granted.

Of course I loved Mike. But even if I'd never met him, I still would've been mesmerized by the thought of an unknown twenty-six-year-old capable of convincing the powerful and legendary Nederlander family to endorse his dream for black artists. The Nederlanders! These people own thirteen Broadway houses and the Pantages and Palace Theaters in Hollywood! Yet he created a fifty-fifty partnership with them and made them his co-producers. Even now we (and they) own the film, video, and television rights to "Checkmate."

During a couple of year-long runs in Los Angeles and on a tour of Equity theaters in San Francisco and DC, as well as on Broadway, the "Checkmate" cast included each of these acclaimed performers at one time or another:

- Denzel Washington
- Ruby Dee
- Vanessa Williams
- Ron O'Neal
- Marla Gibbs

- Paul Winfield
- Roxie Roker
- Carl Lumbly
- Richard Lawson
- Al Freeman

With playwright Ron Milner's amazing script and Woodie King directing, there was obviously no shortage of actors and actresses interested in signing on!

Despite the legal problems that would eventually overwhelm Mike, he invariably made sure that all of the artists involved in the production were treated well and fairly and paid on time – and that their working conditions supported them creatively. Any of them will attest to this truth, and to the fact that "Checkmates" was important to their careers.

And still there was time for one more significant theatrical production, "Stepping into Tomorrow," which starred the daughters of four famous African-American men: Martin Luther King, Jr., Malcolm X, Harry Belafonte, and Sidney Poitier. I'm proud, as is my husband, that the play was well received both politically and artistically.

So I think you'll agree that no one needs to dismiss Michael Harris as just some rap-music guy. As I'm sure you've noticed, he's not one-dimensional. And he's not finished with all the great things he's planned for his life. Not even close.

"Michael Harris is a talented entrepreneur."

– Freddie DeMann,
Maverick Records CEO

Actor Danny Glover and Lydia Harris at a charitable event

Leigh Savidge with Lydia and Michael Harris

Michael and Lydia "Lady Boss" Harris, the entrepreneur

Singer Howard Johnson, Lydia, and Greg Cross

Lifestyles executive Oscar with Dr. Dre

Lydia and Joe Isgro

Michael, Lydia, an attorney, and Mark Friedman

Lydia and Eric Woodley

Lydia and artist Ruff Dogg

Lydia and the Lifestyles crew

Actor Caffeine and Lydia

Lydia, Jonathan Clark, and Andre (R.I.P.)

Tom Arnold and Lydia

SQUEEZE PLAY

We began business as Godfather Enterprises, and we planned to create companies for music and film production in most areas of the entertainment industry. We incorporated in early 1992, and I was listed as an officer and director of each Godfather company and organization, including Godfather Music. David Kenner and another attorney, Sheldon Ellis, handled the paperwork.

Suge Knight was to manage the business, and David Kenner was supposed to draft all the documents needed to start up and run it. A major "supposed to" was the responsibility of properly signing all our key artists and producers, and this was quite a spectacular list. (Imagine Dr. Dre and Snoop Dogg for openers!) Then too,

Kenner was to provide legal defense in whatever criminal cases might potentially apply to Suge Knight or any other Death Row artist or producer.

Of course, entertainment lawyers and criminal-case attorneys don't often wander into each other's territory, but this was a special situation because *we* had people who attracted notoriety. David Kenner or someone like him was crucial for us, and in return for his services I would assist as needed and share my fifty percent of the business with him.

Death Row Records grew out of GF Music, Inc., and again Kenner did the paperwork. The company was launched at a huge bash at Chasen's Restaurant in February, 1992, after almost anybody who *was* anybody had received an invitation that read like this:

NOTICE TO APPEAR

Chasen's Restaurant
Beverly Hills, California
Tuesday, February 25, 1992

You are hereby ordered to appear
before the honorable Dr. Dre
and the officers of GF Entertainment,
as a guest of the court,

to witness the springing of
Death Row Records.

Cocktails/Buffet from 6:00 p.m.
Premiere performances 7:00 p.m.
Multiple giant-screen viewing of
34th Annual Grammy Awards 8:00 p.m.

R.S.V.P. Norman Winter/Associates
(213) 469-3434
Non-transferable

I can still remember what I wore that night. I can probably remember what *everybody* wore that night. It was a rare occasion! But it wasn't a promise of good things to come.

Even though Death Row quickly produced what would be the first in an enviable series of platinum albums, by mid-1994 my own involvement with the company was becoming less and less significant because of a conspiracy between Kenner and Suge Knight (and others, as I would eventually learn). It was a complicated plan, but here's what it involved:

- In April of 1994, Interscope and Jimmy Iovine entered into an agreement with Lifestyle Records that called for the services of Dana Dane.
- In June of the same year, Interscope and Lifestyle entered into an agreement for the production services of Kevin Gilliam, known as Battlecat.
- Interscope, as one of the only record labels involved in urban music at that time, had already signed an exclusive, hugely lucrative contract with Death Row Records.
- All of the Lifestyle Records contracts had been assigned to New Image Media, Inc., another company that I owned and controlled.
- In July, 1994, less than five weeks after signing the Battlecat contract, Interscope terminated its relationship with my companies and assigned Battlecat and Dana Dane to Maverick Records, which was owned by Madonna and which had no experience in the production, marketing, or distribution of urban music.
- Not surprisingly, Maverick did only minimal marketing of the Dana Dane album and then chose not to release Battlecat's album.
- As Maverick should've predicted, Battlecat later released numerous platinum albums, but that first one – and I repeatedly attempted to purchase the

master so that I could release it – was allowed to gather dust somewhere. Maverick never even suggested a price to me.

- I was then blackballed by Jimmy Iovine and John McClain at Interscope and by Suge Knight; and when Battlecat worked with other artists at Interscope and Death Row Records, I was precluded from sharing in any of the proceeds, even though I had an exclusive producer agreement with Kevin Gilliam. The word "shafted" comes to mind.
- McClain told Gilliam that I'd been blackballed, so despite his exclusive agreement with my company, he (as Battlecat) ignored our contract and entered into agreements with many other artists and labels.
- Gilliam/Battlecat and Jimmy Iovine later entered a co-ownership agreement for Aftermath Records.
- I arbitrated my claims in a lawsuit against Kevin Gilliam, and my agreement with him was found by the arbitrator to be valid and enforceable.
- By late 1995, I had received no remuneration from Death Row Records; and each time I spoke with David Kenner about this inequity, he responded that the business was still recouping production costs, that it was operating in the red, that a series of other factors was preventing the distribution of my profits...

- Kenner constantly reassured me that I would be seeing money "soon" and that I should be patient, particularly since a federal probe of Death Row was ongoing.
- I was unaware that Kenner and Suge Knight had incorporated Death Row and that the corporate filings excluded me from serving as an officer and/or director.
- I then decided to develop a video project in documentary form concerning the history, background, and development of Death Row Records. It was to be called "Welcome to Death Row" and was to be co-produced with Leigh Savidge.
- By 2000, most of the footage for this documentary had been collected; editing was taking place; Leigh Savidge was arranging for release; I was working on the music for the soundtrack.
- I contacted a New York attorney, Paul Marshall, to arrange a meeting with Jimmy Iovine for the purpose of discussing the project.
- In June, 2000, I screened the documentary for the people at Interscope, who passed on it.
- By March, 2001, I had lined up an impressive roster of artists and producers for "Welcome to Death Row" and was raising money for the soundtrack.

The movie, minus soundtrack, had already been screened at Big Time Studios in West Los Angeles.

- Artists and producers interested in participating in the soundtrack project included Black Chill, Charlie Mack, Jewell Payton, Ruff Dogg, Snoop Dogg, Black Caesar, Wycliff Jean, Battlecat (believe it or not!), and Dr. Dre.
- Between January, 2001, and August of the same year, when Suge Knight was released from prison, Knight and Death Row Records and its personnel slandered me and viciously dragged my name through the mud.
- On Wendy Williams' talk show, Knight claimed that I was an informant for the government who – in order to secure my husband's release from prison – routinely "set up" people for the Feds. The interview, which stunned me and seemed to come from absolutely nowhere, was nothing but false, misleading, malicious slander.
- Knight's actions (which he calculated and began to carry out while in prison) were intended to disrupt my plan to market and distribute "Welcome to Death Row" and, further, to discourage backers and distributors from contributing to the project.

- In the spring of 2001, Interscope and Suge Knight blocked my attempts to distribute "Welcome to Death Row."
- Suge Knight defamed me on national television, referring to me as a whore, a snitch, and an informant. This slander was part of his obviously determined effort to continue blackballing me in the urban music world.
- Knight's overriding desire was to prevent me from obtaining the industry recognition, power, and funding necessary to claim my fifty-percent interest in Death Row Records.
- After I learned what Knight had said in the media, I immediately called David Kenner, who reassured me that he was still looking out for my interests, and for my company's, and that *I would get paid*. Only then did I fully accept the fact that I would need Kenner's records in order to learn *the truth* about my case. Needless to say, Kenner was not forthcoming.
- On behalf of Suge Knight and Death Row Records, attorney Jeff Lowry threatened to sue the Mann Theaters for copyright infringement if they allowed "Welcome to Death Row" to be shown at the Black Film Festival.
- Between February and April, 2001, Death Row's lawyers sent letters to Blockbuster Video, Holly-

wood Video, and other video rental companies, threatening to sue anyone who distributed the documentary.

Now, I realize what a very long chronology of events you've just had to struggle through, but I want you to understand that I was devastated by Suge Knight's comments. I was literally in shock! I could not begin to understand why someone would create such an elaborate smear campaign. I mean, *I* knew I'd been faithful to my husband since we first met, but *the public* was told that I was a gang banger and had had sex with dozens of recording executives in order to further my singing career. What nonsense! What lies! What defamation of character! I was a featured singer at Death Row's coming-out party. There was no need for me to use the casting couch as a stepping stone to the studio!

Because of Suge Knight's destructive and malicious comments, however, I withdrew into myself. I could not handle the pressure caused by his abusive and premeditated words. Everything I'd ever worked for fell apart. My reputation had been destroyed. My self-esteem was shattered. I was physically and emotionally exhausted. Remember the old thing about how "words will never hurt me"? Not true. Words can do you in. And Suge Knight was *thorough*.

- By calling me a rat and a snitch, he compromised projects that I'd been working on with a number of rap and hip-hop artists.
- By associating me in people's minds with the government, he in effect portrayed me as an enemy of urban music, especially with those artists who had histories of legal problems.
- By making slanderous and misleading statements to the media, he helped chase away potential investors and artists who'd been committed to the documentary project, and I was unable to finish work on "Welcome to Death Row."
- By going on tirades and making public threats, he was able to force me to abandon my participation in the music industry.
- By making it his goal in life to shut down my business operations, he also fraudulently took away my financial solvency. A comparable project introduced into the marketplace in early 2004 was "Tupac Resurrected," which engendered sales of more than a million DVD's and 1.5 million copies of the CD soundtrack. Since a CD soundtrack sells for $14.99, there could have been $6,000,000 in gross sales from the "Welcome to Death Row" CD alone, if I had been able to get the recording done – and the major-

ity of that money would've come to me as producer of the video and the soundtrack.

It's been a hard time because of Suge Knight. It's been a terrible time. I suffered stress and depression, and neither would go away. How do you manage your life when it spins completely out of control? How can you make sense of anything?

Strangely enough, though, Suge Knight was not the only source of my continuing difficulties. Leigh Savidge, my "Welcome to Death Row" partner and co-producer, made a lot of money off my video! He convinced all the cable stations to play it but conveniently forgot that, as executive producer, I was entitled to fifty percent of the profits. What was his motive? Well, what was anybody's? Absolute greed, of course – and, too, some people just seem to see female executives as targets, and I suppose I'm a *very* visible target.

And if I'd been able to hang on? Look out, world. Different story, different ending! And, for the record, *maybe* Death Row wouldn't have crumbled.

From a February,1992, party at Chasen's Restaurant in Beverly Hills, celebrating the creation of Death Row Records: "Special thanks to Harry O."

– Suge Knight and
David Kenner

LISTEN TO THE MAN

"I worked closely with people like Denzel Washington in the beginning, when he was getting his career off the ground. I understand they consider him the Half-Billion-Dollar Man now, but I didn't make him. I just worked with him. I was in a position to help him.

"So that's why we think Lydia's done pretty good too. I worked with her in the beginning of *her* music career as a manager, as well as putting her in Broadway plays, in circuit plays. I helped a lot of people, but nobody talks about that. Everybody talks about Death Row, and I think that all the talk may have affected people. But, to me, Death Row and Rap-a-Lot are insignificant in the realm of things.

"In the East Side of Los Angeles we grew up hustling because we had to – not because we wanted to. We had to support our families. We had to support ourselves. We didn't do it just for the glamorization of it, and that's what I mean when I say that people need to understand the difference between reality and bullshit. This is something we did not choose. This is something that was available to us. I'm not saying I did the right thing, and I'm not saying that everything I did was wrong. I'm saying that I am just one person who believes that power never sleeps.

"When people talk about Godfather, the reference is to me and Suge, but it was actually me , *David*, and Suge. And David was my lawyer at the time. We had gone past the criminal issues, and we were thinking about doing movies and stuff – you know, different projects: a movie of my life, movies of other people's lives, you know, movies based on David Kenner's criminal experience, movies about people he had represented. That's what we talked about.

"And that's when David really started fishing into the entertainment industry. Then I hooked up with Suge, and we all sat down at the table. Suge was in a lot of trouble at that time, and I felt that David could assist him. And I felt that Suge could assist *us* because he had obtained Dr. Dre's initials on a production agreement.

And I guess that, at that time, Suge had run into some bad luck, and he needed my financial assistance. And I felt that, based on all of our philosophies and our networks, we could make something real powerful.

"Now, my wife Lydia is a very special person. She's the type of person that will do whatever it takes to make things happen. She has stayed with me through the good, the sweet, and the bad. She's as real as they come. She's a Texas girl with a lot of heart who believed in me and believed in a dream. She believed that I would come home again and that we could make a difference. And I just think she should be given a chance to be dealt with based on her hard work and not be connected to the Death Row situation..."

"I'm a workaholic. I applied myself. I know I did wrong in the past, and I am paying my debt to society. That, however, in no way negates the fact that I was blessed with entrepreneurial talent. I could have sold bottle tops and become a millionaire, but instead I made that fatal choice which has haunted me and my family ever since. My deepest regret in life is that I sold dope."

– Michael Harris

STRANDED

David Kenner always knew what he was doing. I mean, he got Tupac off! But he didn't get Michael off.

Maybe he just really has to *want* something in order for him to pursue it. Regardless, I'm convinced that Mike's case was winnable except for David's greed (and his obsession with Veronica!). The miserable truth is that Death Row no longer needed my husband after the company got off the ground, or no longer *thought* they needed him, so it was just a matter of convenience to leave him sitting in prison.

Any pile of money seems better looking when you're getting half of it instead of a third.

...AND IF I HADN'T MARRIED THE GAME

When I was a little girl growing up in Texas, did I dream of how my life would be when I grew up? Was I sure I'd meet my knight in shining armor someday? Did I have happily-ever-after in mind?

Of course I did. I think all little girls believe the fairy tales about Cinderella and Snow White. I think they want to be rescued by Sir Galahad or a cowboy or at least the guy next door, even when they have no idea what they'll need to be rescued *from*. Everything may not be exactly like Ken and Barbie, but there's always that romantic notion.

Well, I've had my adventure. As far as great love stories go, mine has often been the stuff that romance novels are made of. But what sets my story apart from the rest is the fact that romance is *all* I've had. The *day-to-day* part of love is of course what I've been missing all these years. So what I dream about *now* is all those routine, average, ordinary moments that other people take for granted. I haven't had a standard life.

Now, if I hadn't stumbled into the strange and dramatic existence that I've been living since 1988, there's no doubt in my mind that some things would've been different. I wouldn't have had glamorous moments in the spotlight or dangerous moments in the shadows. I probably never would've seen the inside of an internationally known recording studio – *or* the inside of a federal prison. I almost surely wouldn't have handled enormous amounts of money, done business with felons, or been called a whore on national TV. And I wouldn't have had to protect my daughter from her father's business associates.

And yet the Lydia of this life would've been the same Lydia anywhere else. That's because my character was formed long before I met Michael Harris, and nothing that I've experienced in life has been strong enough or smart enough to separate me from myself.

With or without the game, I still would've tried to do right. I would've been singing somewhere, somehow. I probably still would've been a success in business – though I could've just followed my earliest instincts and decided to cook for a living! I would've been true to my husband because that's the way I am, and I would've worshiped God and thanked Him every day for my beautiful child.

And if my time and energy hadn't been centered on my husband's conviction and incarceration, I might've had time to focus on a few things that would've meant something extra to me. I'm *sure* I would've eventually found myself doing some motivational speaking, volunteering in the community, and spending time *only* with people who were good to me, people who could be trusted. And I would've had my child living with me, so that she could've taught me *at least* as much about life as I could teach *her*.

I don't regret the life I've lived, but, yes, I can imagine doing things some other way. I can imagine life without the game.

THE BUZZ

Since I've been back home in Texas, my husband hasn't been thrilled to have me so far away from him. Yet how long can a woman wait outside prison walls? I've finally and at long last had to tell myself that I must live *while* I wait, so here I am – with my family, with my history, with myself.

All these past years seem to have been filled with people talking at me and about me, people on the fringe, people wanting to walk through me to get whatever it is they think I have, wanting to get to the music and the money.

I tried to help everybody I could. When guys who'd known Mike in prison would be released – and I mean serious felons, killers sometimes – I'd hire them. I'd give them jobs at Lifestyle for as long as they could hold it together, and then they'd relapse...because every one of them would end up back behind bars.

One young guy, Evans, stayed with us for two years, which was a very long time for these folks, and he was so fond of me that he called me Mom. Eventually, though, the police came for him – something about a possible murder charge — and he allowed himself to be picked up rather than hide out and cause further trouble for me. That may have been the closest anyone in the industry ever came to doing the right thing for me. Sad.

Later on, though, Evans must've forgotten his gratitude and affection for me because, once he was out on bail, he disappeared, and he hasn't been seen since. Unfortunately for me, I had put up my house as bond for him, and I lost it because of my misplaced trust and kindness. As usual in my life, I was doing unto others as I hoped they'd do unto me, but instead they did me in.

And it doesn't stop there. Back when Evans was picked up and charged with murder, David Kenner, who had planned to adopt the guy, took me down to the police station to...what? I never really knew. To add moral support? Swear to Evans' character? Hold somebody's hand? But what happened – after Kenner left me there! – was that the police decided I could direct them to Evans (which of course I couldn't), so they held me. It was Valentine's Day, Kenner had gone home to "check on" his wife, Evans was nowhere, Mike obviously was out of reach, and there I sat. *That* was a miserable holiday. *That* had people talking.

Sometimes the word was good, though. It's been said on more than one occasion that "if Lydia Harris had been running Death Row Records, Death Row Records would still be up and operational today." Or "if it wasn't for Lydia and Michael Harris, you wouldn't have heard of Snoop Dogg. You wouldn't have heard of Tupac." I've been told that we opened the doors for West Coast rappers and then put the West Coast on the map. And I believe that.

Sometimes people in the know admit that there are men who're so competitive that they won't let a woman get a fair break. They admit that a woman like me isn't often given credit for helping build the foundation of anything major. And most or at least many of the people I've met in the music industry haven't been trustworthy. They haven't had my best interests at heart, and they've seemed to be looking out for themselves at the end of the day. *They* are what have made this long ride so exhausting. There will always be men – and some women – who try to step on a woman with power. They have to be argued with and fought man-to-man, and I haven't wanted to do that. I've wanted to do right.

People have tended to be very negative about my marriage, and when Michael's name has come up, they've been willing to go way back in time to make a point. It's amazing. It's nothing to read or hear even today about the Compton, California, neighborhood he grew up in (twenty-five years ago!) or that it was run by the Bloods. Yet why not focus on a more recent villain? David Kenner lives in a walled-in mansion in Encino, surrounded by cameras and iron gates. His life today is a direct result of his law career and his client list, which has included organized-crime figures and wealthy drug dealers almost exclusively. Is he not *at least* as interesting as we are?

State and county corporate papers back up our claims that Godfather came to life in 1992 and was *my company* when it merged with Death Row. As a prisoner, Michael was not going to be able to run things hands-on, and that sad technicality put me behind the desk, and I was able to do quite well with it. Mike had a dream of being in the entertainment industry, and I had a dream of being a singer, and *our* dream became Godfather Entertainment. We were partners, and at first I was assisting him, and then I was more than his arms and legs because I was also quickly developing my own mind about how to do things.

I want to say (and most people never bother to hear this) that Michael Harris had a true desire to give back to his community, make a difference, and use his money to help young African-Americans achieve things they couldn't have managed on their own. Because of his imprisonment, everything had to be done the hard way, but he did not want to stop *trying* to make things work. He's without doubt an unusually talented man and a great motivator, but obviously the reality of his day-to-day existence has gotten in the way of what he'd intended to do, so he's counted on me to do much of it for him. And sometimes I've succeeded, and sometimes I haven't been allowed to succeed, and sometimes I've finally just had to say, "That's not for me." I've been Michael's arms and legs, but now I also need to be my own – and maybe my own wings as well.

When Death Row opened its doors, Dr. Dre was already famous as a genius in the business, and he was without doubt the most talented producer. So, yes, we wanted him with us. He helped us establish a professional standard far above that of the gangsta rap of the day and even made rap acceptable in places where it had never before been played. He gave us the reputation of being able to annihilate any other label, and for a while that reputation was absolutely correct. Everybody wanted our talent and our success (and, unfortunately, there were plenty of people who didn't care what it took to get either or both).

Once I began working at Death Row, lots of changes started taking place. I made it a better environment, and I think that the people there began to see what a woman's touch could do. With me, things were better looking, better running. I handled meetings with some huge names in the business, from Freddie DeMann and beyond, and I honored Michael's dream, our dream, every day. That's why I absolutely know that Death Row would've become the true empire it was destined to be if greed hadn't entered the picture. But by 1994 "Marion Knight" and "Andre Young" were the only names on the corporate documents, thanks to our attorney David Kenner, and I was stepping back and away and wondering why so few people could be trusted.

There's one guy who hangs around the periphery, hangs around the fringes of the business, hangs around me, and I mention him only because he's like many other people we've known since 1991 or 1992. What gets him out of bed in the morning? I suppose we could say he's a wannabe – but who exactly does he wanna *be*? Sometimes he seems a lot like David Kenner, and then he'll claim his allegiance is to Mike. He'll say that he wants to stay to close to me because he loves and admires me, yet he seems to report to Suge Knight about everything I do. Isn't that too much wandering around and too many loyalties? I think so.

At least with David Kenner I have no doubts. Through the years I've *had* to come to understand him, although the education has been a costly one.

In the past, David has ignored requests from the media to talk about his connection to all those many criminals, but it's no secret that lots of famous people know him – and pay him well. Mike considered David to be even more of a villain than Suge was in all our problems because he felt that David was more manipulative than he looked. Suge was more obvious about it, but David was shrewd. As a friend of mine once told me, David *could've* played it straight. Even in the middle of all those people fighting over Death Row Records, he could've played it straight. He could've said, "Michael and Lydia Harris founded this business with Suge Knight." But instead he slid the paperwork and the business out from under us and holed up in his big, lovely house with all the security cameras. He is a *very* smart man. He understands politics, he knows judges, he's been a prosecutor, he has an impressive vocabulary, he can smile at all the right moments – and he's not troubled by his lack of a conscience. And did I mention how much money we earned for him?

But he was made for a good old boys' club, and of course I wasn't. I don't like winking at people and going behind other people's backs and doing the opposite of what I've said I would do. People who've known me and worked with me, people without ulterior motives, will tell you that I could run *any* type of company. I'm a people person, but making the hard decisions doesn't bother me, and I can hold my own against anybody. I don't even let the huge egos crumble me. But when I was at Death Row and then at Lifestyle, I was definitely different from most of the big shots in the industry because I would keep my word. I would tell you if I could do something, and I would tell you if I *couldn't*, and either way I'd be telling the truth, and then I'd follow through. I haven't met a lot of *men* who will admit that they can't do something, but none of that bothers me because I just want to do the best work I'm capable of, or that anybody's capable of, and then I also want to be able to live with my conscience when I go home at night. I believe that David Kenner doesn't have to worry about such things.

In our business it was important to be able to recognize talent early, and this is something that I did with Battlecat and others. I had the vision for that. Also,

I kept up with everything and everybody in the office, whether I was in L.A. or Houston or anywhere else I needed to be, and even though we had a lot of executives on the payroll at times, I was in charge. But I believed in having a humane environment for people, and that's why I was never too busy to listen to their problems (even though maybe I should've been), and I would help them find somewhere to live or get their apartments set up for them or whatever they needed. All of *that* was part of the business for me. I stabilized an unstable company and some very unstable people. I had my own production deals at Interscope and Maverick. I was my own person. And still I didn't exist in the minds of some folks.

I've been through a lot of lawyers in the battle to reclaim what was stolen from us by David Kenner, Suge Knight, and others. Some of them I'm sure were bought off, but others just didn't want to touch the case. They didn't take me seriously, they didn't like the sound of "Death Row," they were afraid. Definitely, some of them were afraid. An attorney I've been working with recently, someone who *finally* believes in our cause, says that he's " very angry" that other lawyers left me with a mess. "The time in which lawsuits can be filed is a very important consideration, and many other lawyers had turned down the case because the parties involved were very powerful, and some of them had the reputation of becoming violent. And rather than do the right thing and protect her interests, most of the lawyers simply passed on the case. And others had given her bad advice and let the statute of limitations run out." This man thinks that my case deserves to be heard. He thinks that *the system* owes me that much. Imagine!

Of course, our case is different from any run-of-the-mill lawsuit because of the extreme personalities involved. In a situation like this, people are intimidated and afraid to get into the fight. They feel jeopardized. And so they don't speak up, most of them. That's one reason that I've often been on my own. *Thank God for the law firm that's working with me now.*

People tell me that I should be holding seminars for women whose men are in prison. They say that "behind every successful Black man is a Black woman." They like it that I've held onto my dream without becoming hard-hearted and that I still want to help folks even though so many of them have mistreated me. But my favorite image of myself has to be the one where I've been compared to a cork, of all things. That's because, no matter how many times it gets pushed down, that cork keeps bobbing its way back up to the top of the water and figuring out new ways to swim.

Married to the Game

If people want to talk about me, let them describe me that way.

MAKING GOOD

During the past ten years or so I've helped nurture the careers of Snoop Dogg, Dr. Dre, Battlecat, Ruff Dogg, Dana Dane, and many people from prisons and from the streets that nobody else would've spent five minutes with. I believe I can live with that.

"You're only as good as the talent that you discover, and she has discovered some great people. Lydia has several business qualities, actually. She's strong-willed. Very strong-willed. She's a boss, she's an executive, and she conducts herself like a boss should. If Lydia had been running Death Row Records, it wouldn't have been just a million-dollar business. It would have been a billion-dollar business. Let's clarify that: not with an "m" but with a "b," for *billion*.

– Greg Cross,
Lifestyle Records

TESTIMONY

"This man has tried to ruin me more than anyone will ever know. By many threats that I've received, business opportunities that I've lost, and the outright lies told about me, my reputation has been damaged beyond repair. This man has even lied about me during legal proceedings.

"Mr. Knight, through his evil financial empire, has wanted me either hurt or killed. He knew that I was there in the beginning of the ordeal to witness the creation of the monster, both man and label.

"People in the business world were and sometimes still are afraid to deal with me because of my affiliation, or *ex*-affiliation, with Mr. Knight. In the beginning, Mr. Knight and I were friends, I thought. He even used to refer to me as his little sister. I never suspected how things would change – especially how Suge Knight would change, for the worse.

"No one in this courtroom can fully understand the embarrassing pain caused by Mr. Knight's inferences that I was someone who slept around. I've never been that type of person and will never stoop to that lowest of lows, not even for money – *especially* not for money.

"I just want to get this over with and behind me so that I can move on with my life. But for the record let me say that I was always under the impression that I would be compensated for my previous involvement with Death Row Records, which began at its inception.

"Mr. Knight and his associates thought that I was dumb and naive and would just roll over, lie down, and die. But God is my protector from the evil that men do."

WHAT MONEY WON'T BUY

Recently a guy I barely know telephoned me from out of state to ask if I wanted him to send me some money. Money for what? So I could drop everything, turn my back on my family and my business and my life, get on an airplane, and fly down there to make him "happy" for a while.

Of course, I told him no. "Why not?" he asked. "If it's not money that turns you on, what *does*?" Well, what turns me on certainly isn't *him*, is it?

And this kind of thing happens all the time! Some guy will think that he can buy me. But guess what? I'm not for sale. Maybe I've needed money sometimes, maybe I've been worried, maybe I've felt alone, but I have never, *never* been broke enough or worried enough or lonely enough to do anything promiscuous, and I never will be.

Besides, my family and my business and my life are *much* more attractive to me than that guy is.

THE EVOLUTION OF ME

I believe that women can make a difference in this business. Most people may not realize it, but there have always been strong women, very talented women, behind every situation (Sylvia Rhone comes to mind), and I hope I've been one of them. I *know* I've been one of them. Didn't start out for this, wasn't programmed for this, but here I am.

Of course, home for me was Houston, where I was born and raised – and it's the place I've returned to. Back then, before Los Angeles and the entertainment world meant anything much to me, Bennigan's was the place to be on a Friday night. If you wanted to see anybody, that was the spot, and that's where I used to see *another* Kim, the one who was also known as

"Choice." She was a rapper for Rap-a-Lot Records, but when she was in town, she was always at Bennigan's, and that's where I got to know her.

So she called me on the phone one night and said, "Remember the guy I've been talking about? He's in town. And I know you're tired, but you gotta meet us at the club."

And she was right: I was tired, but I guess I was a little bit curious too because I went to the club – and the first person I saw there was Michael Harris. Now, I didn't know who it was that I was supposed to meet, exactly, and I certainly didn't know it was *this* guy, so I just started on down the stairs, maybe with a little bit of an attitude. And he said, "Hey, what's your name?" And I said, "Lydia," but then I just kept walking to where all the girls were hanging out.

Kim was sitting there, so I asked her, "Where's the guy that you wanted to introduce me to? I came all the way over here for this?" And she said, "I'll go get him." And of course it was Mike. And I said to her, "That same guy approached me when I first walked into the club." Then Mike pulled out a hundred-dollar bill and said to Kim, "Hey, can I buy your girlfriend a drink?" And I told him, "I don't drink." And Kim said, "Just get a 7-Up. We know you don't drink, so just get a 7-Up." So he bought all the people at the bar drinks. So I said to the bartender, "You gonna give him his change back?" And Mike said, "I don't want it. Keep the change."

So I'm saying to myself, "That was probably this brother's last hundred-dollar bill." But I said to Kim, "He's cool, you know." And she said, "He wants to take us out of breakfast." But I said, "You *know* I've got to go to work in the morning, and it's already 1:30." But then he walked outside, and they pulled his car up, and it was this black Mercedes Benz SEC convertible. So she said, "Are you gonna go with him?" And I said, "Yeah, right!" But to myself I said, "This is my dream car!"

When I met Michael, he exposed me to another world. I'd always visualized that kind of place, but I never thought I'd ever be there. Just meeting Mike, just that moment, showed me a totally new lifestyle. Upscale, you know. Just completely different from what I was used to. Different people with different ways of handling themselves. Little things, like opening a car door for me. My old boyfriend in Houston had never opened the door for me! So that little bit from Mike just said a lot. Even if he was driving, he'd come around to open *my* door, and that meant something to me. He made me feel like I was somebody. He made me feel special – really special. He was that kind of guy.

Now, meeting him didn't make me forget where I'd come from, didn't make me forget my focus in life, but he gave me something that I'd needed to be exposed to, something that I never would've had if I'd stayed where I was, if I'd stayed home from the club that night, if I'd never set my sights any higher.

I remember Michael saying to me one time, "If I gave you a hundred thousand dollars, would you have my baby? I want a son." And I said, "No, I couldn't have a baby for money. I'd want to raise my own child, and the father and I would have to be married." And he said, "You wouldn't have my baby for a hundred thousand dollars? You'd be the perfect one to have my baby for me." But I said, "Well, I couldn't do it. Maybe you ought to give somebody else the hundred thousand dollars." He was serious about it, though!

When I started going to court for Michael, I just sat back and listened and observed. And during the trial I really saw for the first time who Michael "Harry O" Harris really was, but somehow I managed not to dwell on Harry O. I just concentrated on the man I'd met in Houston, the man who opened car doors for me and chose me out of all the other girls and wanted me to have his baby. I didn't look at him for what everybody else said he was about. I didn't think about what he did. I just looked at the man I'd met, and that's what made up my mind to say, "Okay, I'll marry him."

I went to visit him every weekend for thirteen or fourteen years. Unless I was sick, which didn't happen very often, or unless I was home visiting my family, I was there for him. Every weekend for years and years. I knew some other women who were also attached to prisoners, and we'd meet in Oakland and then rent a car so that we could drive the rest of the way. Then we'd get a hotel room where we could take a shower and get ready and be at the prison by Saturday morning. Then all of that got to be too much, so I rented an apartment in Pelican Bay. And we'd stay there on the weekends – four girls, four ladies waiting for a visit – and the others wouldn't have to come up with money for rooms. They'd come stay with me in the apartment, and we'd just make the whole thing like a vacation. I know this sounds impossible to most people, but that's what we did: we just made it like a vacation. We'd buy groceries and cook dinner, and then we'd go for our visit, and then we'd pack up our bags, go home, and get ready to do the same thing all over again . It was a vacation. That's how we managed it. We made something out of nothing so that our lives wouldn't seem as depressing as I guess they really were. I made his world *my* world and his life *my* life. And I never complained.

I never complained about the visits. I never complained about what I had to go through for those visits, about what I had to wear. I had one wardrobe for meetings and work and an entire separate wardrobe for the visits. And that's just how I lived! I actually looked forward to visiting every weekend. The life didn't stress me out, and in fact I couldn't wait for the next weekend to come. Amazing? Maybe. But for me it was normal. And I *did* get pregnant with Michael's baby after all, and then we got married, inside Lancaster State Prison. He trusted my judgment about the details, which he still does, and I got all the paperwork ready, and we were married in the jail cell by the same judge who'd sentenced Michael to prison. And I'm here to tell you we were happy to be married.

Funny – the doctors had always told me I couldn't have a kid, so it was really shocking when I got pregnant, and in prison! And right after that, the prison stopped conjugal visits for lifers, so I know that my child is an angel, a gift from God to keep me going. She's special. A month after she was conceived, in 1994, the prison stopped the family visits. *Timing is everything.* Amazing.

When I told Mike I might be pregnant, he kept telling me that he'd been sick, that *he* was throwing up. And I told him, "But you know I can't be pregnant! You know the doctors told me I can't get pregnant!" And he just said, "I feel funny."

So I had a pregnancy test, and that came out positive. And I kept that bottle right beside my bed over the weekend, and that little pink line never had a circle in it, and I was like, "Wow!" And I went to see a doctor. And I was three weeks pregnant, and the doctor told me to come back to see him every week because I had endometriosis, and I wasn't supposed to be able to have kids. And I spent a lot of time seeing the doctors, and they kept a close eye on me, and sure enough I had a healthy baby. A miracle baby.

Now, the marriage I have isn't anybody else's idea of normal. We're married according to the paperwork, but physically we're not together. Our marriage has the words and the commitment, but we never get to do anything together. We've *never* done anything together. So I don't know how any of that feels. I don't know if I'll ever have that feeling. I just know how to cope with what I've got.

So, from prison, Mike started dealing with different lawyers, working on his case, and we were always on the phone talking about it. And one day I was doing some song for him, and he said, "Oh, I love your voice! Would you like to be a singer? I have a couple of producers I could hook you up with."

And he hooked me up with Jonathan Clark, a guy who managed a group called The Good Girls. And

Jonathan introduced me to Giorgio, who had a studio in his town house in Carlton Square, and Giorgio got one of his producers, Keith Andy, to do a song with me called "Wishing You Were Here." So I let Michael hear the song over the phone, and he said, "I like that!" And he was talking to a man named Eric Whitley, and Eric said, "Mike, I've got this guy, Suge Knight – he's a bodyguard for Dr. Dre. You know, maybe he could hook Dre up to do a remix with your girl. So I'll introduce you to him." And that's how it started.

Mike and Suge spoke on the phone, and the next day I met with Suge at Solar Studios. He said, "How much money does your husband have?" Well, of course, I wasn't there to talk about my husband's money. So he said, "If he's asking Dr. Dre to do a track for you, then evidently he's got *something*. I'm just trying to give you a good price because I respect your husband." Whatever! But anyway, he introduced me to Dre, then to Walkie Stewart, Glove, Provoke, and Lonely. And he said, "These are some guys that I've got on board. Let Dre hear your song." And I did, and Dre said, "Yeah, I think I can do you a remix on that." So, the next thing I knew, Suge and Mike and David Kenner were all having a meeting, and then we were in the music business almost overnight.

When we started Godfather Entertainment, Michael would always say, "Lyd, make sure you always document everything – you know, keep records of everything." And at the time I didn't know anything about anything, really, so I just followed his directions. What paperwork I *didn't* keep, David Kenner had on file for the company, as part of a good-faith arrangement with us. But if I'd ask about anything, Kenner would always say, "Lyd, don't worry about that. I've got that paperwork in the safe." And I'd say, "Okay," and I never tripped over that situation. And when Kenner would go down to visit Mike at the Metropolitan Detention Center, he'd have all the paperwork with him, so Michael would have no cause to worry. In particular, Kenner had the paperwork showing our ownership of Godfather Entertainment, so we felt comfortable about that. And David would just say, "Okay, I'm taking it and putting it in the safe." And at the time I didn't know how important that paperwork was. And David Kenner never gave me a copy of it, but *he had it*! And now it's been destroyed. Now nobody claims to have any memory of it at all.

The same day as the coming-out party at Chasen's, Michael was moved to Tehachapi State Prison. When that happened, he lost touch with Suge and Kenner for about a month and a half. And during those six weeks,

Kenner started making all kinds of moves. He started acting all strange with me. But of course I didn't know why. And I also didn't know why, on our extremely important debut day, the prison system had coincidentally decided to move Mike. I'm sure you know what I'm saying. We had had plans to have a speaker phone set up for Mike so that he could almost be at the Chasen's party. And then none of that could happen for him.

So when they told me he'd been moved, I just took to my bed. And everybody who called me that day said, "Lyd, you've got to get up here and perform! If you don't, you're really going to disappoint Michael." And I said, "I don't know if I can do it" – because it was such a shock to have him moved so suddenly, and on that special day. And I said to David, "Why did they do it"? And he said, "Lyd, I don't know." And he was all worried about what I might do, and he said, "I don't know if you should get up there and perform. You know you could mess up if you're thinking about Mike." But I said, "I gotta do it *for* Mike. I gotta get up there and perform." And that night, David stood up and, with a straight face, toasted the man who had made it all happen: "Harry O."

Kenner and Michael had a very involved, very active business relationship. With Kenner and *me*, it was a different kind of interchange. I just made the phone calls for Mike and did what I needed to do for David. During much of the time that he was Mike's attorney, I was convinced that he was the guy who would be getting my husband out of prison. So I was always saying to myself, "He's the one who can do it for Mike and me, so just let me make sure that I tell him everything that's going on in the company because he can protect our interests."

And I thought that Kenner needed to know, for his own sake, that Suge didn't care for him, even though all of us were supposedly working together, and I would tell him, "You need to look out because Suge doesn't like you." And David would always say, "Let me hear him say that!" So even though I probably shouldn't have done it, I made a three-way phone call and, unbeknownst to Suge, let David hear what he had to say. And from then on there was a big change.

David must've told Suge what I'd done, and then Suge didn't feel that he could trust me any more – and Suge was really looking for *somebody* to trust. Also, when Suge feels that he can't trust you, he's through dealing with you. So Kenner had made sure he put the thought of distrust into Suge's head – which is odd because it was *Suge* who was making negative comments all the time about David, and I was just the messenger. Before then, David Kenner had just been the guy who was paid to keep Suge out of jail. Now, though, the two of them got a lot closer. Really, really odd – and some of the strangest of all the strange bedfellows.

So David forgot all about Michael, even though he would go through the motions of visiting him in prison. And when he was there, he would always cry (about Veronica sometimes, I'm sure), and he'd say he was sick and worn out with things, and Michael would have to comfort him because Michael is all emotions. Besides, the visits kind of served to keep Michael from suspecting what was really happening with our company. They distracted him from the reality of how he had already been abandoned. Michael would be thinking, "Here's the man who can get me out. He's really powerful and knows what to do." And all *Mike* could do was believe him — but *I* had lost my belief in him. And I would be thinking, "How can Mike trust this man, when he goes to the prison acting one way and comes back out totally different?" And Mike couldn't see it. But when I'd been around David, I'd seen both of his personalities and all of who he was.

Suge, of course, signed with Interscope, and I didn't know anything about the deal or about the company until Michael read about the whole disloyal thing in a newspaper. And when Suge and Kenner visited Michael and told him about the situation, they must've come up with a good enough story to get by with because they kept dealing with him — and they kept freezing *me* out. And I knew that I would never be allowed to play a truly major role in the business, so I created my own company and called it Lifestyle Records.

In 1993 and 1994, Lifestyle was doing well. We had signed some real talent and were creating a name for ourselves. And I remember that time especially because I was pregnant. When I was eight months along, though, I got a phone call that forecast the beginning of the end. Maverick was going to drop our label because Madonna didn't want any gangsta rap associated with her company. Of course, we didn't do any gangsta rap, but nobody was listening to us by then. And everything was falling apart.

Loyalty is a strange thing when it isn't *true* loyalty – when it's got dollar signs attached to it. And I think that's what happened with us. Lots of people we'd counted on were no longer available to us. Maybe we didn't look like winners any more; maybe someone "got to" our people; regardless, every day became a big struggle. We had managed to surround ourselves with some people who believed they deserved and even needed more than we could provide. They were going to the highest bidder, and I guess that wasn't us.

So both of our companies were blowing up, and, on top of everything else, I had to contend with the separation from Mike. And there were also the people who placed themselves in the middle of our lives without being invited there. They just saw our *dis*advantages as advantages for themselves, and *our* misery became the right time and the right place for *them*. There are plenty of birds of prey in the music industry, and sometimes I think I've known most of them.

So everybody started hating everybody else. It was like having a stack of dynamite in a room, and somebody decides to blow it up. And in our case, Suge lit the match. Oh, it wasn't as if Suge and I fought. I always tried to keep a cool head, especially around him. But I admit that we had words after my baby was born in 1995.

I called Jimmy Iovine one day and said, "Hey, I'm Lydia Harris." And he asked why I was calling him. So I answered him, "I just want to let you know that I'm a partner with Suge Knight in Death Row Records." And he said, "I checked the corporation's papers." And so I said, "I just want to let you know that we're partners." But he said, "I *still* want to know why you're calling me!" And I kept trying: "You're a distributor for Death Row Records, so I thought you should know!"

Anyway, right after that useless conversation, I got a call from Suge. I don't know whether he was on a three-way or not, but I wouldn't be surprised. And he said, "What's up, Lyd?" and I told him, and we had words. So I guess Suge got upset, because he called David Kenner's office, and David got Mike on the phone too, and Suge said, "Your girl talks real bad, and you need to check her for talking that way." And Michael called me to ask what I'd said to Suge, and he told me not to be talking to him like that. But I said, "You know, he doesn't need to be talking to *me* like that, and I'm not going to bow down to him!" And I suggested that the three of *them* needed to be communicating.

I have to say, though, that Suge scared me. I had a house out in the Valley, four or five blocks from David Kenner's, and I really didn't hang with anybody then. I was pretty much alone. But David and Suge knew for sure where I lived.

Well, one morning I had to go to the beauty shop, and I transferred my phone calls, and sure enough the phone rang when I was in the car – but it was a hang-up. Then I realized that I'd forgotten something, and I had to go back home. When I got to the house, though,

I saw that the alarm was off, so I ran back out to the car and called David. And I said, "David, somebody's in the house!" And he said, "Lyd, what are you talking about?" And I repeated, "There's somebody in the house!" And he just said, "There's nobody in the house." Not "I'll be right there" or "Call the police" or even "Be careful!" – just "There's nobody in the house." But I said, "The alarm box is open, and I can see drawers out on the floor. There's somebody in the house!"

So I drove over to his house and told him, "Come on! Let's go over there and call the police!" But he just sat there for forty-five minutes, probably, until his wife Linda finally got a gun out. And he said, "What are you doing?" And she said, "Let's go see what's going on. Somebody's in the house." So we went back over there and called the police. And when the policeman arrived, he went through the house and came out again and said, "Ma'am, somebody was in your house."

So once it was safe to go in, we walked through the house. And even though somebody had been there, the place hadn't been broken into. Somebody had used a key. And the whole place had been ransacked, and the shower door was all busted up, almost as if the intruder had been disappointed or even angry that I hadn't been there, almost as if somebody had *expected* me to be there. So I said to David, "You need to call Michael." Of course, Mike was in Tehachapi then, and he could get the use of a phone only once every three days or so. And David asked me, "What am I going to say to him?" And I said, "Tell him what happened! Right?" And he was *very* hesitant to make the call.

So when Mike got on the phone, the first thing he said to David was, "I hope Suge didn't have anybody break into my girl's house!" And David said, "Why would you say something like that, Michael?" And Mike said, "I'm just saying it!" And then David got really nervous, so he asked, "Michael, why would you suggest something like that? It's just strange to think that somebody would want to break into Lydia's house." And Mike said, "I'm just throwing it out there. But, you know, I don't want Lydia going back to the house! So what're you going to do for her?" And David said, "Lydia can come live with us."

And I moved in with them – not an ideal situation, but at least I didn't have to be alone any more. Anyway, I'm thinking that the invitation to move in was David's way of showing Mike that we were all still together, even though we weren't, of course. It was his way of calming Mike down and diffusing the situation, of saying, "Okay now, I've got your wife here at the house. Don't worry. Trust me."

While I was there, though, it wasn't as if I was treated like family. Instead, I was treated like somebody off the street who needed a place to stay. And when I'd visit Mike, I'd tell him that I had to find another place to live because they had this big dog, and when I needed to go into the bathroom, I'd have to call David on the phone to get the dog away from the door. I told him it was almost like being in prison. And Mike said, "Damn, I hate that you're living like that!" And I said, "Yeah. They have a nice house, but the dog is crazy. You know, even when they put him outside, I still have a problem because then I have to call David if I want to go out." It was like they were keeping tabs on me.

And then when Suge was coming over, David would say, "Lyd, go sit somewhere for a while, okay? I don't want Suge to know you're staying here." And I'd say, "Why not? We're all a team!" But David would say, "He just doesn't need to know where you're staying." So I'd go to the Red Lobster at Reseda, and I'd sit there until David would call me and say, "Okay, Suge is gone." But I'd have to sit for hours because Suge would always be late. And one time Mike called me and said, "Where are you?" And I told him "Red Lobster" and that I'd been sitting there for three or four hours. And he said, "Why?" And I said, "Because Suge's at David's house, and David says he really doesn't want Suge to see that

I'm living there." So Mike said, "I'm going to call you right back."

So then he called David and made *him* call *me* on a three-way. And Mike said, "What the hell you got my wife sitting up there for? Forget Suge! Let her go back over to the house! You know what's going on, and you and Suge need to get down here and visit me, man." And David was like, "Oh, no, Mike – it's nothing!"

So then David had me go on back to his house, but after that he'd still more or less lock me up in my room, and I'd have to park the car where Suge couldn't see it so he wouldn't know I was there. So I told Mike, "They tell you *one* thing, but then they react a totally *different* way around me. I gotta get out of that house!" You see, at the time that those guys broke into my house, there had been a safe in the guest bedroom, and they'd pulled it out onto the floor. I guess they thought there was money in it, but actually there had never been any money in it, partly because Suge was always worrying about *what was in that safe*! And I'd kept telling him that there was nothing in the safe. But looking back on everything, I can definitely remember how obsessed he was with the safe and what might be in it. And he also knew that I had a rottweiler that wouldn't let anybody touch me. And when the house was broken into, they shot my rottweiler (and left my other two dogs alone). And I don't think any of this is a coincidence.

And so I went home to Texas. And while I was there, Mike called to tell me the Feds had been at the prison. He said, "Lyd, tell Kenner to come here and visit me. There's people here asking questions, so tell him I need to talk to him." So David went to talk to him, and after that Mike called me again, this time to say, "Baby, I'm going on a visit with David. I'll call you when I get back." He wasn't sick, and there was nothing wrong with him. He just had to make this "visit." And of course I had no idea what was going on.

So four or five hours later I received another phone call – this one from the prison counselor saying that they'd had to take my husband out in a wheelchair because he'd been taken sick. And I said, "Sick? I just talked to him, and he wasn't sick then! He said he was going on a visit with David Kenner. None of this sounds real to me!" And I called David to tell him that Mike had been taken sick, and he showed no concern whatsoever. But I asked him, "Wasn't he okay when you visited him earlier?" And he said, "Yeah, he was fine." So I just kept calling the prison. And they would say, "Sorry. For security purposes, we can't give you any specific information. All we can tell you is that your husband is okay." And then I got upset and said, "Something isn't right!"

So I knew I had to do *something*. And I called the prison counselor because he and I had developed a good relationship over time, and I said, "Are you sure Michael's okay?" And he said, "I can't really go into details, but he's not doing very well." And I said, "Well, do I need to fly out there? Do I need to take the baby – you know, for Michael to see?" And the counselor said, "Well, where he is, we can't let you see him. But I'll keep in touch with you to let you know if his condition improves." So of course I was a nervous wreck.

And the counselor called me back – on Thursday, I think – and he said, "I think you need to come visit Mike. They're bringing him back to our facility, and I just think it would be a good thing if you could come for a visit." And I said, "Is he dying?" And all he could say was, "I think it would be best if you came to see him, but don't bring the baby." So I made all the arrangements for taking care of things while I was away, and then I got on a plane and went to see Michael.

When I got there, they brought him out in a wheelchair. And when he saw me, he started crying, and, you know, his mouth was all twisted, and he couldn't walk. And I was saying to those people, "What happened?" And they said, "All we know is that your husband and

David Kenner were talking, and Kenner got him a 7-Up, and after that Michael didn't know who he was. And that's when the doctor was brought in to check for cyanide poisoning."

And I raised a tremendous amount of hell, and I told them, "If Michael dies, you're going to get sued!" So then the facility let the doctors in, and they were talking about Guillain-Barre syndrome and saying that he would've died for sure if nothing had been done for him. And after that, David Kenner didn't visit Michael again, and maybe that's why my husband is still around.

So my life's been like that: a struggle to be believed, to be taken seriously, to make sense out of a terrible nonsense, to protect my family and my name – and sometimes a struggle just to stay alive. Now, when we started thinking about the Death Row story, I couldn't have predicted that it would turn into "Welcome to Death Row." At first, of course, it was just a concept about what had really happened in the industry, what Michael Harris' perspective was, what Lydia Harris' perspective was. But then I met Leigh Savidge, and he was the guy who came up with the name for the video. Mike and I had simply wanted to get our story told. We'd wanted to make sure we'd investigated every piece of information and put all the evidence out there because, as you've seen, there've been plenty of people interested in obscuring our history with Death Row. There've been plenty of people who wanted the music world to believe that Michael and Lydia Harris had never happened.

When I met Leigh Savidge, I'd been involved in the industry for more than a decade. I was co-founder of Death Row Records and had achieved success for a lot of people through my other two companies, Lifestyle Records and New Image Entertainment. I'd worked with an impressive number of artists and producers in hip-hop and rap music. And then I became co-executive producer of the docudrama " Welcome to Death Row."

Now a major lawsuit has been filed on my behalf. The targets of this suit are the industry executives who consistently and dishonestly conspired to prevent me from furthering my career in the industry and who also maliciously separated me from monies to which I am rightfully entitled. I'm seeking royalties and other profits owed to me by my former attorney David Kenner, by Kevin Gilliam, also known as Battlecat, and by others, and I'm suing Suge Knight for defamation of character and to set the record straight. And I've not had an easy time through any of this.

How I've consoled myself through all these years of struggling has been through prayer, of course. Even when I've been at my lowest, I've never been truly alone, just as none of us are ever truly alone. If we place ourselves in God's hands, we can be sure that we're doing the right thing and that He will fulfill us. He'll find a way to happiness to us. I'm a believer in God and in His plans for us, and I have no doubt that my faith is why I'm here today telling my story.

And my central focus now, even beyond the business and the legal battles and Michael and me, is to make sure that I can take care of my daughter. That's my main goal, beyond today: to make sure that she has everything she needs in life, including a decent education, that she knows what she *wants* from life, and that she never has to undergo some of the stressful, exhausting, heartbreaking things that have happened to me. She should have better. *We* should have better.

So, yes, I've tried to do right, and I've listened to my heart and my conscience, and as a result I've been controlled by my feelings. My emotions have ruled my mind – so much so that I now sometimes ask myself if I even know what love is, if I'd recognize it if it came to me again. And how will I learn to trust anyone? There's been so much sacrifice! So many people have taken advantage of me, and why? Have I deserved this? Have my family members – my mother, father, brother, daughter – deserved to lose themselves in my life? What about the drastic toll that my *husband*'s life has taken on all of them? Have they been sacrificed? Have *we*? Are we prisoners too?

Yet at the end of the day, at the end of this long legal war, and even at the end of my life, I will at least know that I'm an independent woman who can stand on my own feet, guided by God and my own good intentions, and confident that my self-respect is intact. Life can knock me down, but it can't keep me there. And I still have things to do.

"I was Lydia Harris' executive assistant. I helped her run a company called Lifestyle Records. We had a record company that I think had the best talent in town. There wasn't a lot of gangsta rap. It was what I would say was very tuned-in poetry. I saw our artists as troubadours of today's common man.

– Bonnie Bellville

ALL MY CHILDREN

First there was Godfather Entertainment, and then...

- Death Row Records
- Underground Network (UGN), a record distribution company signing independent labels and producers
- Keeping the Dream Alive (KDA), a music and film production company
- New Image Entertainment, a record label
- Lifestyle Records
- Dream-On Productions (DOP)
- "Welcome to Death Row"
- *Married to the Game*

Think I don't know the business?

TAKING OFF THE GLOVES

As long as I've been in business, people have mistaken my kindness for weakness and tried to play me. They've had ulterior motives. They've given me pain without noticing my strengths. They've stacked the odds against me. But they haven't known me.

It's incredibly difficult to be taken seriously when you're a black female in the corporate world; and when you're a black female in an incredibly high-pressure, high-profile, high-stakes industry, forget being valued for yourself. If it weren't for my husband, in fact, I might never have met *any* male who was truly impressed with the interior me.

Behind the scenes at Death Row, Rap-a-Lot, and Godfather Entertainment, I learned that I could be innovative, fearless, and ambitious – and I managed to deal with guys who were ruthless and sometimes violent. Regardless of my quiet Texas background, my continuing love affair with Michael Harris led me into a community of impatient and threatening men who were mostly unaccustomed to thinking of women as partners, equals, or functioning human beings.

As Michael's wife and as "The Woman Behind Death Row Records," I more or less inherited his so-called street support team. That was the easy part. The *hard* part was persuading his guys to work with me, and I also had to earn their respect, which I eventually did. Later, though, when things got vicious for me, I had to hire trained security people to protect me because most of the street guys don't feel any *true* loyalty and because ex-cons can't legally carry firearms. The days of a street "family" are over!

As a woman in charge of several companies, many male employees, and a frightening amount of money, I never let my power – or whatever that power was perceived to be – go to my head. I never misused my position, and I'm totally comfortable saying that. Now, some people seemed to hate me anyway, just for the sake of hating me – especially those men who were learning how unapproachable I was. In fact, they created campaigns to discredit me and nicknames to insult and belittle me:

- The Godmother
- The Performer
- Lady Boss

You name it: they tried it.

There was a lot of plotting behind my back, a lot of attempted sucker punches; and, as usual, no, I'm not feeling paranoid. But I've been the target of so much character assassination that I'd be forced to laugh if the whole thing hadn't been so deadly serious. I've had to roll with this real-life ride!

Imagine a big, crazy room where many chess games are being played simultaneously, always with you facing a nameless adversary. Imagine that, if you don't make a move, someone will make it for you. And imagine that, nine times out of ten, you'll be at a disadvantage. In that imaginary situation you wouldn't sit still, would you, waiting to be rescued? No, you'd quickly learn *a lot* of strategy. Chess is a war game, after all, and the player is responsible for all of her moves.

After so many years of drama, so much intrigue, I could've been completely bitter. Instead, I've been the one constant of my own life. I've stood by Michael, tried to be a good mother to LyDasia, and kept my head out of the constant uproar. Being real, never giving up (never!), and fighting for what's fair are the essence of *me*. They define Lydia. If people today want to be reassured that there actually are strong black women with indestructible Christian values, invincible family ties, and the ability to stay the course while embracing lifelong dreams, I invite them to think of me. What other people consider impossible doesn't have to *be* impossible for you – or for me. And as to those many people who didn't want me to succeed? They didn't get their wish!

When speaking to women's groups or to female prisoners or at universities, I want people to hear my story. I want to give them some of the optimism that sustains me, some of the strength to overcome. Maybe Michael and I will never ride off into the sunset. Maybe a storybook ending won't be written for us. But I can promise you this, without the smallest doubt or reservation: I'll be a faithful and supportive person, as I always have been, and I'll keep my head and my faith up high. And I'll do it for my daughter and for whoever needs to know that there's someone like me out there.

All it takes is a velvet touch – and an iron will.

Executive producers Lydia Harris and Leigh Savidge at a New York City screening with supermodel Tyson Beckford

RED Sony distribution executives Cliff Cultreri and Allen Grubic with Lydia

California governor Arnold Schwartzenegger and Lydia at a benefit event for children

Howard Johnson, Lydia, and background singers

Lydia and BoyzIIMen

Debbie, Lydia, attorney David Kenner, and Evans at Dr. Dre's Chronic Album party

Rap/hip-hop legend Dana Dane, Lydia, and MJJ artists

Mike, Lydia, and Suge Knight

Battlecat, BJ, CJ Mack, and Dub C

Battlecat and MJJ artists in the studio

Howard Johnson and Lydia performing

Darrell, original director of "Welcome to Death Row," with Lydia, Jeff, and Joe

WORDS TO LIVE BY

Dignity. Loyalty. Integrity.

WORDS *I'VE* LIVED BY

The same.

AND, AT LAST: REVELATIONS

On March 9, 2005, in Los Angeles Superior Court, Judge Ronald Sohigian awarded me $107 million in damages. My own attorneys had cautioned me not to expect more than $10 million.

Of course, the games that lawyers play are always mysteriously off-limits to their clients. Unless you're unusually smart and aware, your life will be callously tossed around by people who'll charge you huge sums of money to do exactly that!

I was a pawn in the hands of many, many lawyers through the years. And, since I'd always been encouraged to *trust* lawyers, I probably made it very easy for those particular con artists to cheat me. After all, I certainly tended to do as I was told.

During this recent lawsuit, for example, I was urged not to appear in court. Now, this advice seemed strange to me because, in the past, my legal representatives had always insisted that I show up, even though I would've preferred to be almost anywhere else. So I prayed and analyzed the situation and decided that I'd been deceived entirely too many times before. I vowed to have myself one hundred percent present for *anything* that pertained to me.

Later on I discovered that these officers of the court and defenders of the American Way, these knights in shining armor, were in bed with the other side. I had been discussed, my case had been discussed, and all of my privileged information had been discussed. Deals had been made. I hadn't even been told about offers to settle out of court! It was the ultimate insult: to be treated like someone who was trespassing in her own life.

So I fired my lawyers, and an impossible burden was suddenly lifted from my shoulders.

But what ultimately happened? Well, I believe that justice finally had its day. I believe that all those years of being true to myself; of believing in God, our dream, and, yes, my husband; of standing up again, time after time, when people and circumstances had knocked me down – I believe that this beautiful, amazing, but very strange life which was created for me (and which I struggled against terrible odds to maintain) at last evolved into a reward that no one, including me, could've predicted...and I'm not talking about the money. It's the vindication of my name. It's the verdict, *in a court of law*, that Lydia Harris is exactly who she's always claimed to be. It's the small, quiet voice that says, "Well done!"

Sadly, the end of the battle has also meant the end of my marriage. After so many years of looking at each other from the outside in and the inside out, after arranging our lives around prison schedules and courtroom dockets, Michael and I have reluctantly admitted that "we" no longer exist. Thank God, then, for our miracle child. We'll always love her, always parent her, always celebrate her. She's the good that came from all the bad. She's the very best part of both of us.

Through it all, of course, I've never been truly alone. God has kept me company, and He has also given me a mother, a daughter, a few unwavering friends and family members, and even – in the end – one lawyer who believed in me, went to work for me, and won for me. For all of them I'm everlastingly grateful.

As for the dark times, when hope was sometimes very difficult to hold onto, God gave me His words, which sustained me. In the book of *Revelation* he said, "Let the evildoer still do evil, and the filthy still be filthy, and the righteous still do right, and the holy still be holy. Behold, I am coming soon, bringing my recompense, to repay every one for what he has done. I am the Alpha and the Omega, the first and the last, the beginning and the end. Blessed are those who wash their robes, that they may have the right to the tree of life..."

No one on earth can ever truly erase those words from my heart.

ACKNOWLEDGMENTS

First and foremost, I must give honor and thanks to God, who is the head of my life!

With gratitude to my family and friends:

Margaret and Burley Robinson, my parents
LyDasia Harris, my daughter
Michael Harris, LyDasia's father
Cedric Robinson, my brother
Irene Goodie, my grandmother
Nana
The Jordan family
The Nicholson family

Ronald Robinson
Jerne Murray
Cheryl Mitchell
Eric Woodley
Greg Cross
Mark Friedman
Jim Coleman
Randy Morgan
Kevin Black
Andree Caldwell
Nikki Carter
Dana Dane
Ruff Dogg
Jewell Payton
Terrance "T-Rolli" Ball
Geraldine Turner
April, my favorite photographer
Terri Woods, Literary guidance
The staff of LeReve Hotel, Los Angeles
And Ken Nettles

In loving memory:

>   Robert Goodie, my grandfather
>   Pinkie, my friend and life coach
>   Trecee, my friend

Married to the Game

And Jeffery Nicholson,
who played a major role in my life

Spiritual thanks:

Yolanda Adams
Juanita Binder
Paula White
Joyce Meyers
T.D. Jakes
And many others!

This last group of people have accompanied me on my daily walk with God. Their preaching, teaching, and music on TBN and Daystar have helped me grow as a person and as a Christian.

LYDIA HARRIS

It's said too often, but sometimes it's true: "it ain't over till it's over." Well, my life isn't over. My story isn't over. Join me soon for Act II.

ABOUT THE AUTHOR

Lydia Robinson Harris owns a small restaurant in Texas, dotes on her daughter LyDasia, believes in God and family – and has spent most of the past two decades living a life that the rest of us would have a very hard time imagining.

As the wife of convicted drug dealer Michael Harris, she once divided her time between courthouses and prisons, a series of elegant homes in California, and her office at Death Row Records. For a small-town girl of simple tastes, she managed to survive some amazing extremes!

Nothing prepared her, though, for the darkness and ugliness she would encounter when ruthless people (some of them famous, all of them wealthy) decided to squeeze her out of everything she had. From rumors to lies to malicious slander to death threats, her name and reputation were hauled through some particularly dirty waters.

She admits that she was too trusting. She knows she tended to look on the good side of folks. She had a habit of believing what she heard. Now, though, *now* she's been educated. Now she's seen reality. Now she understands what it takes to maintain her sanity, her composure, and her faith in a very greedy world.

And now she's ready to start over again – on her own.

THANKS TO:

Front and back cover photography by April L. Reed
Unique 4 U Photography and Graphics
www.unique4uphotos.com
713-668-4242

Front and back cover make-up stylist
DramaFre On-Site Services
832-752-2518

Ken Nettles, author's creative consultant
starplanner@comcast.net

*Note: a portion of all proceeds from book sales will be donated to The Lydia Harris Literacy Fund.

L B Publishing

www.marriedtothegame.com | www.lydiaharris.com

Order Form

To order additional copies, fill out this form and send it along with your check or money order to: L B Publishing, 14019 S. W. Freeway # 599, Sugarland, Texas 77478, Book Price $18.95, S & H (Via US Mail) $3.50: Total $22.45.
Order with Visa or Master Card:
Card#_____ _____ _____ _____
Valid through date: Month____ Year____
Please allow 3-4 weeks for delivery.

Ship _____ copies of *Married to the Game* to:
Name:_____
Address:_____
City/State/Zip:_____
___ Check for signed copy

Please tell us how you found out about this book.
___ Friend   ___ Internet
___ Book Store   ___ Radio
___ Newspaper   ___ Magazine
___ Other _____

L B Publishing, a DOP Investment Group

* A portion of all book proceeds is donated to the Lydia Harris Literacy Fund: "Unconditionally Educating the Youth of Today in a Caring Way."